I0511352

Dan Larkin

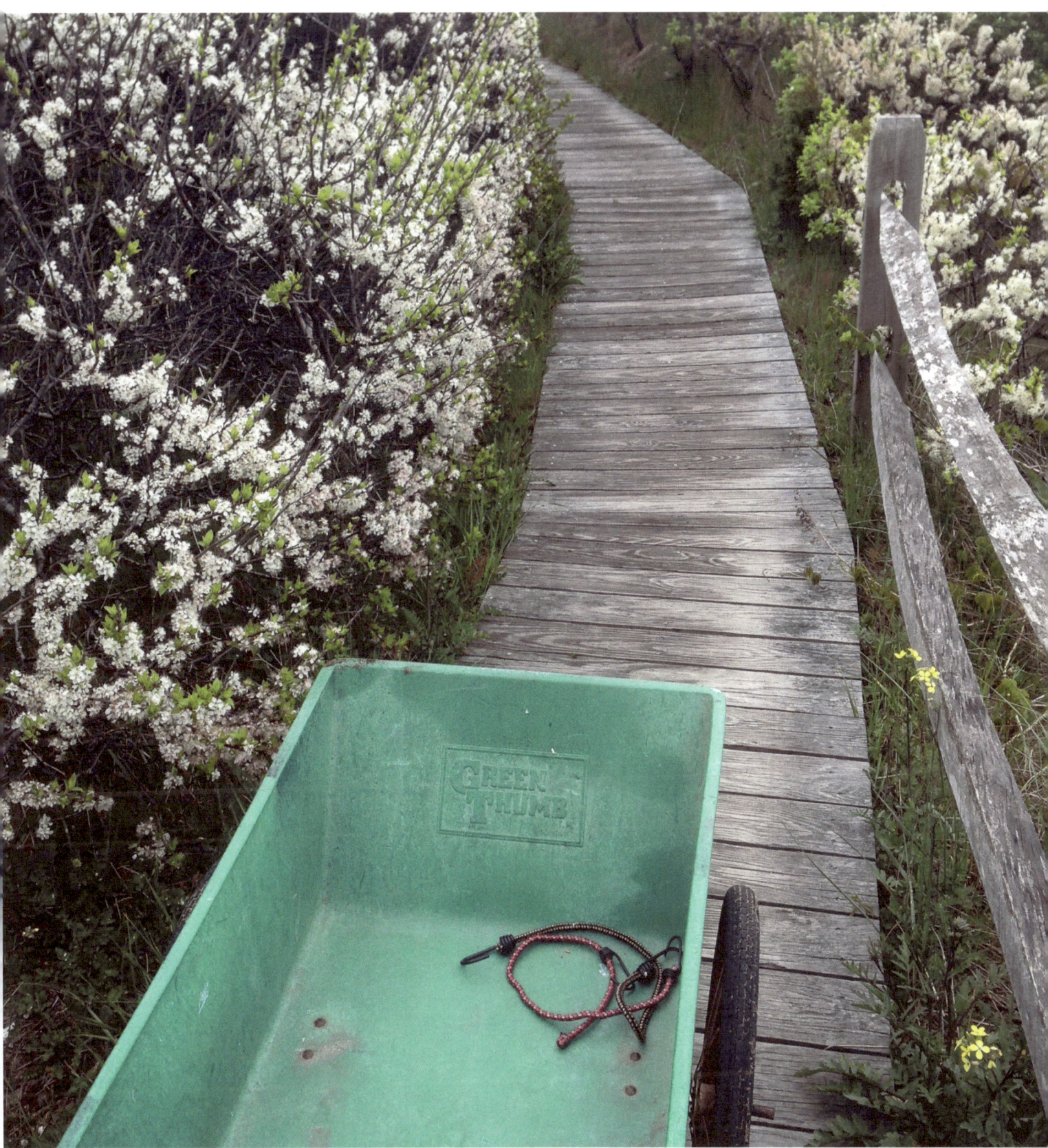

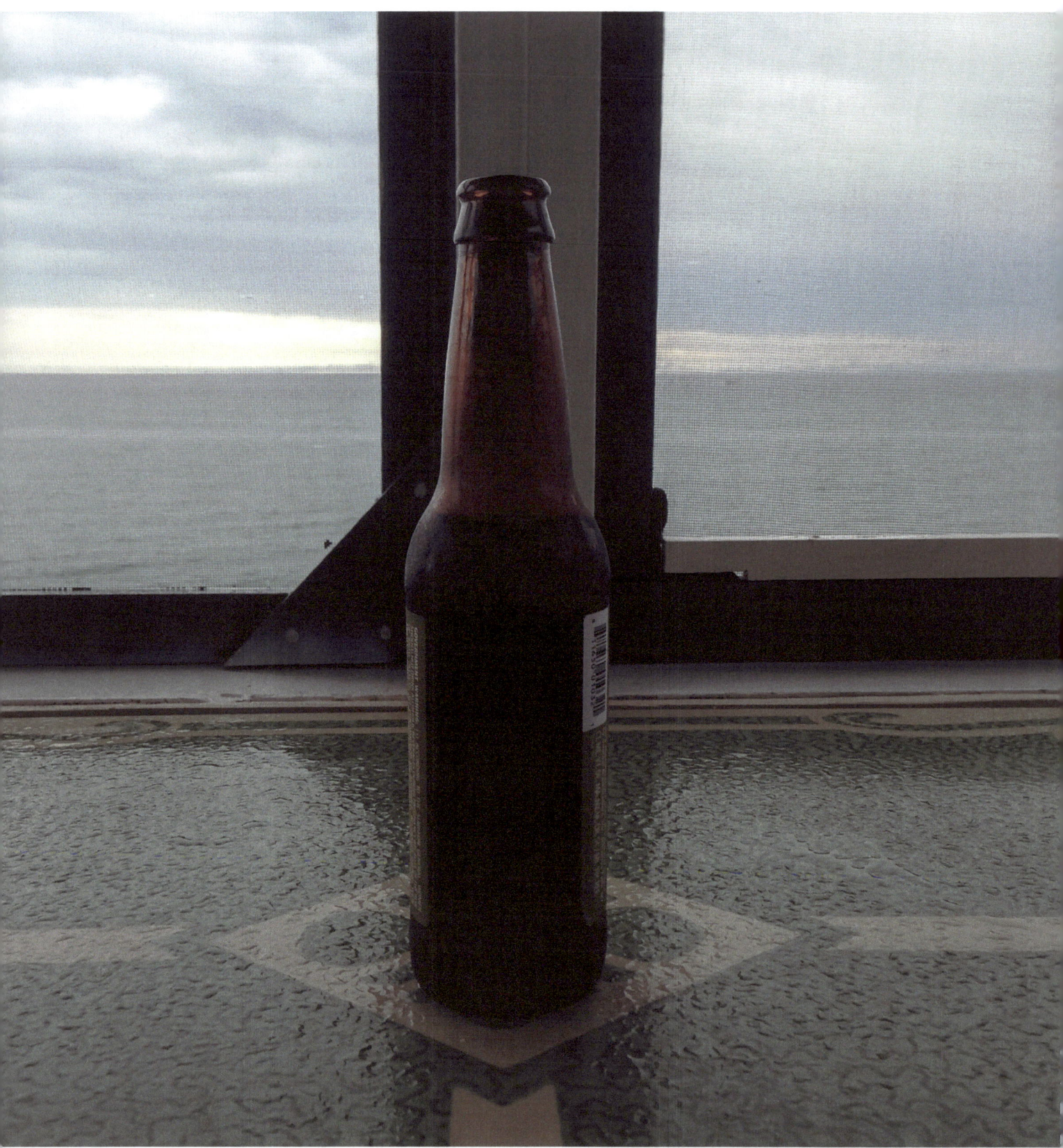

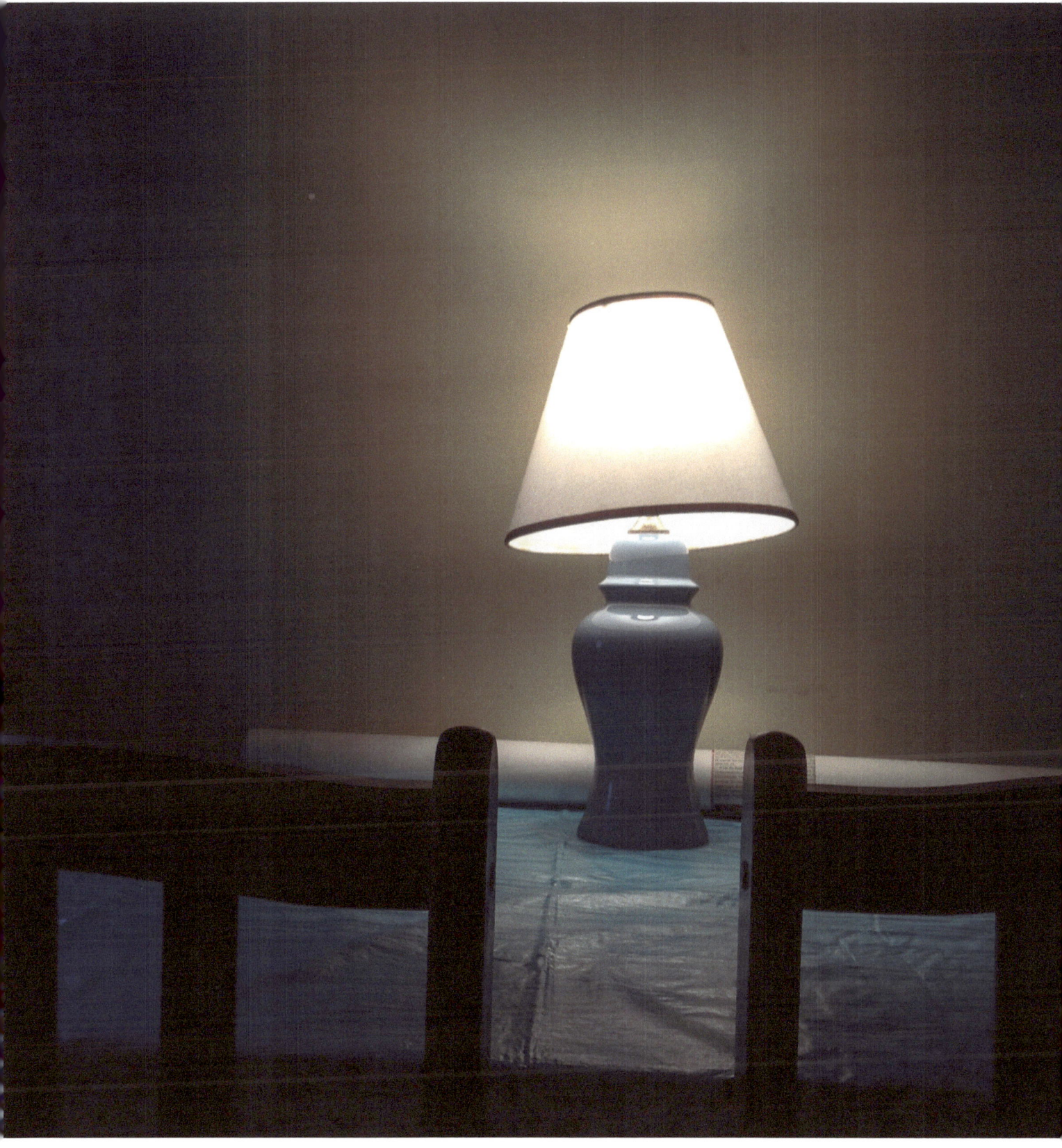

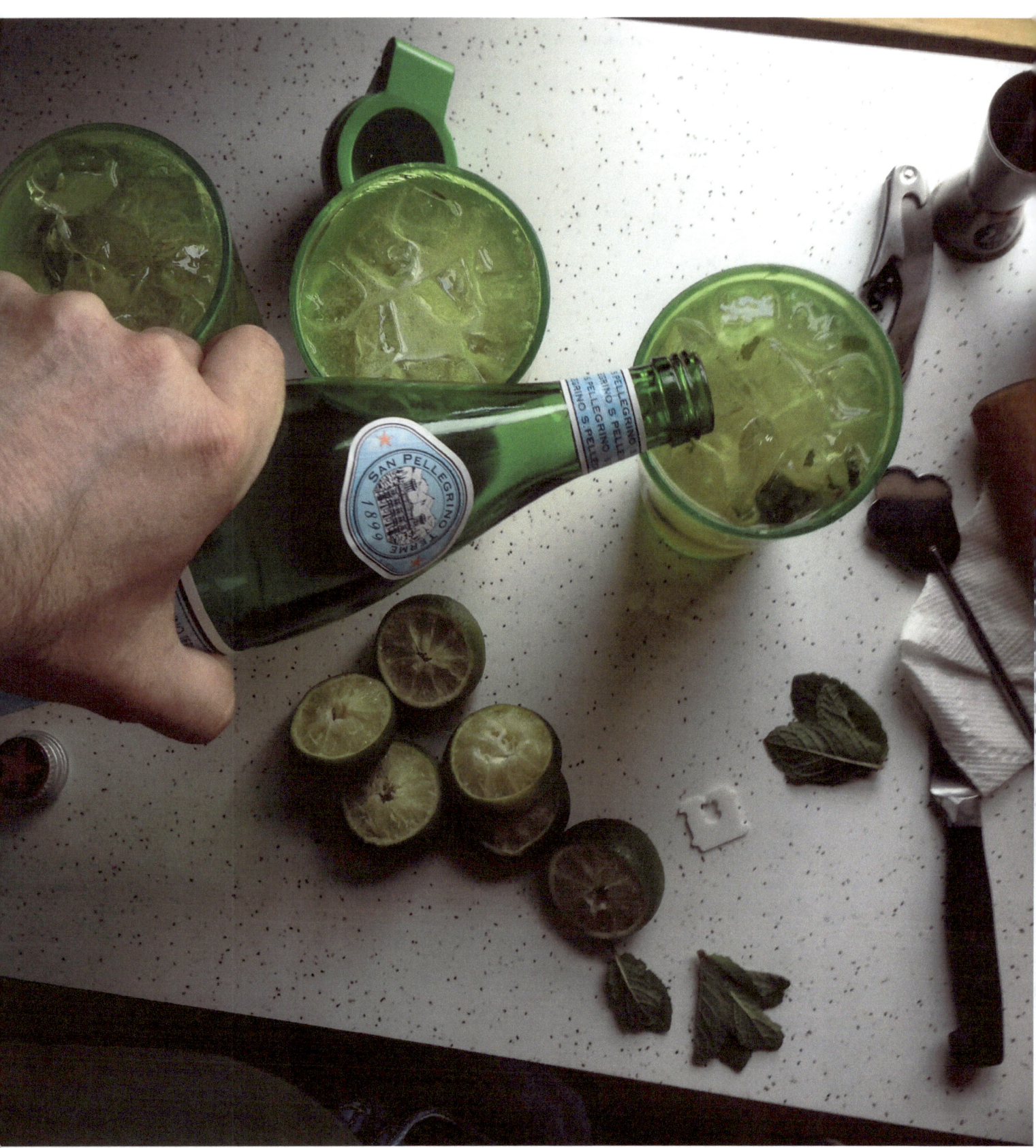

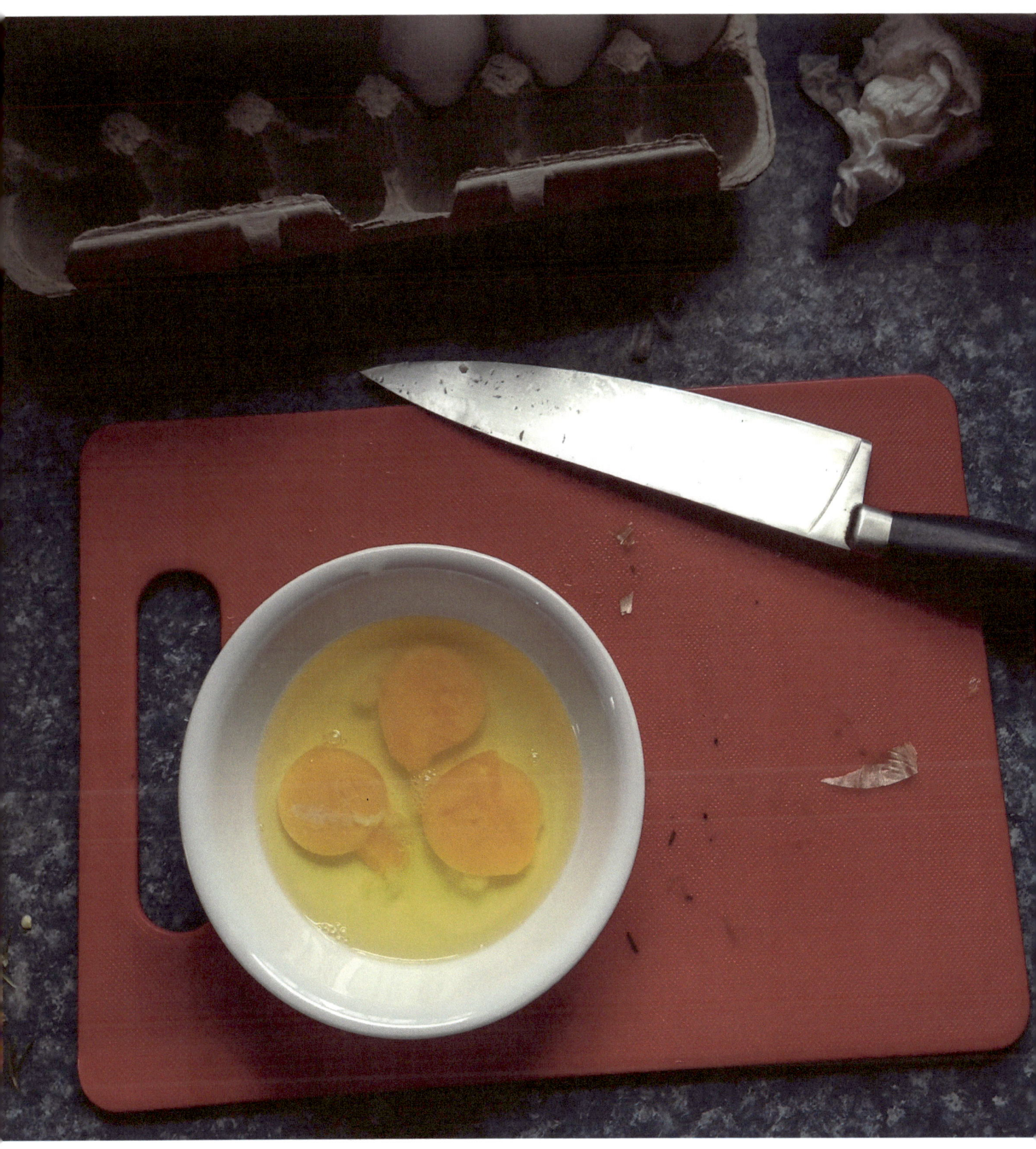

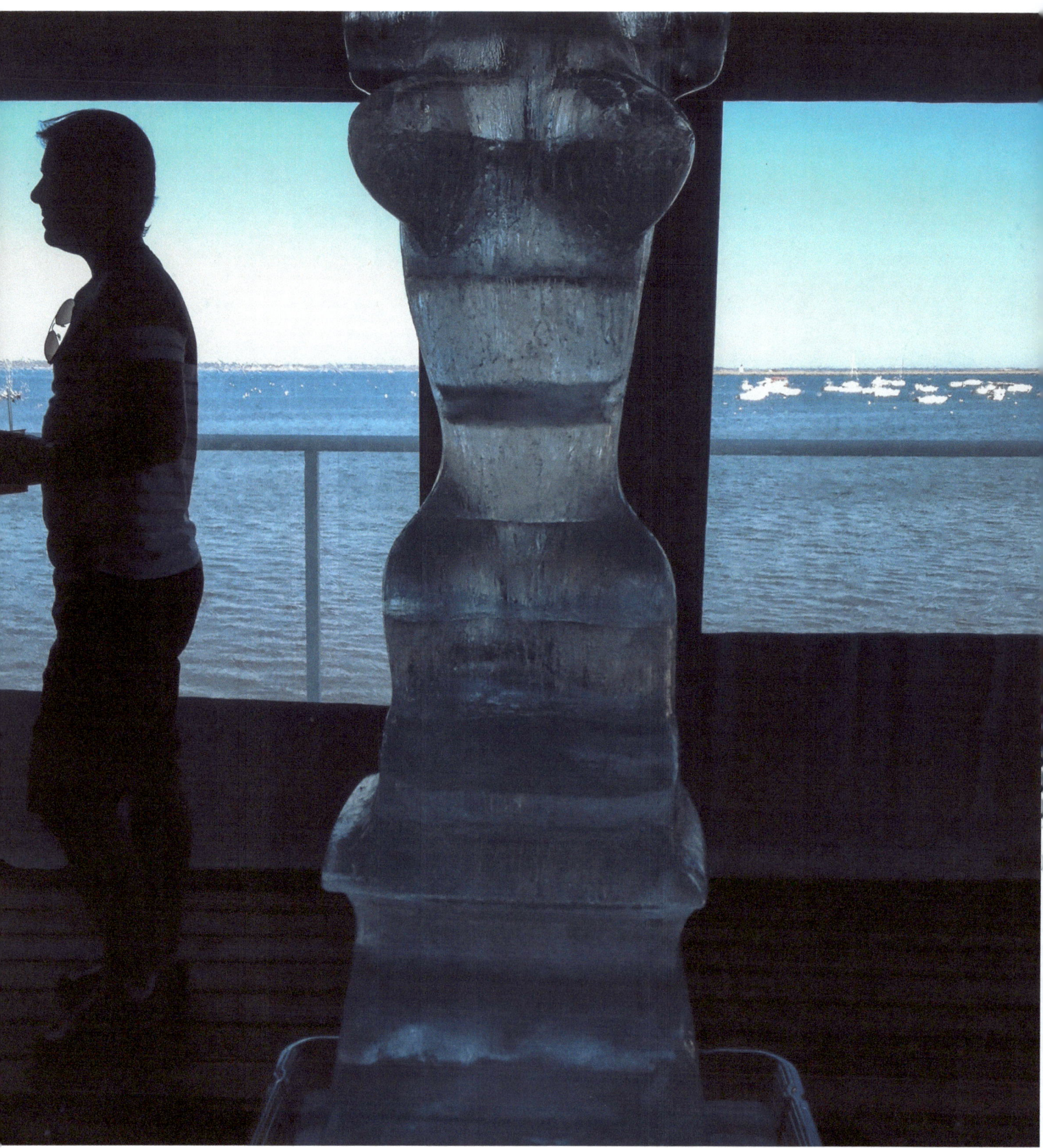

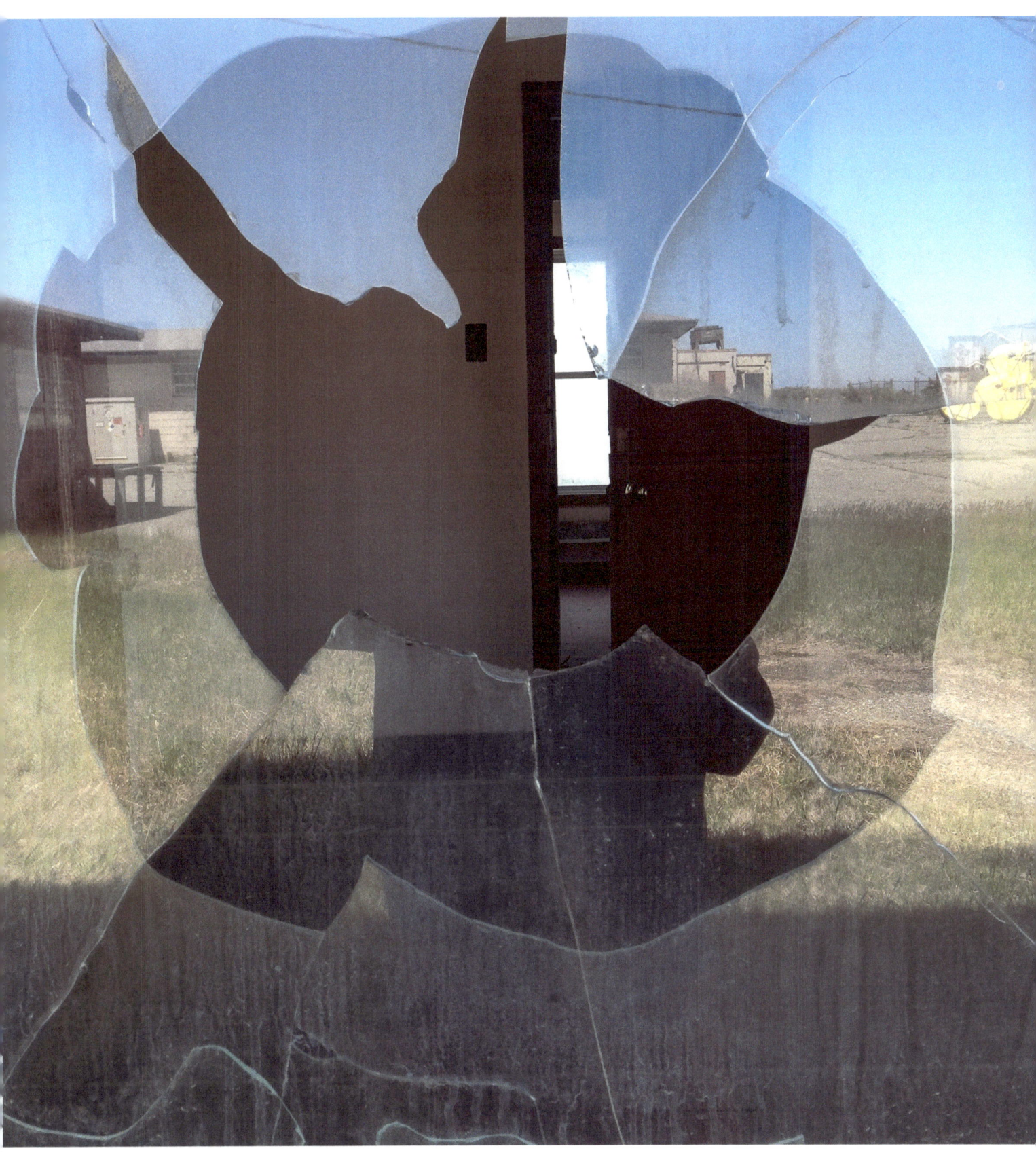

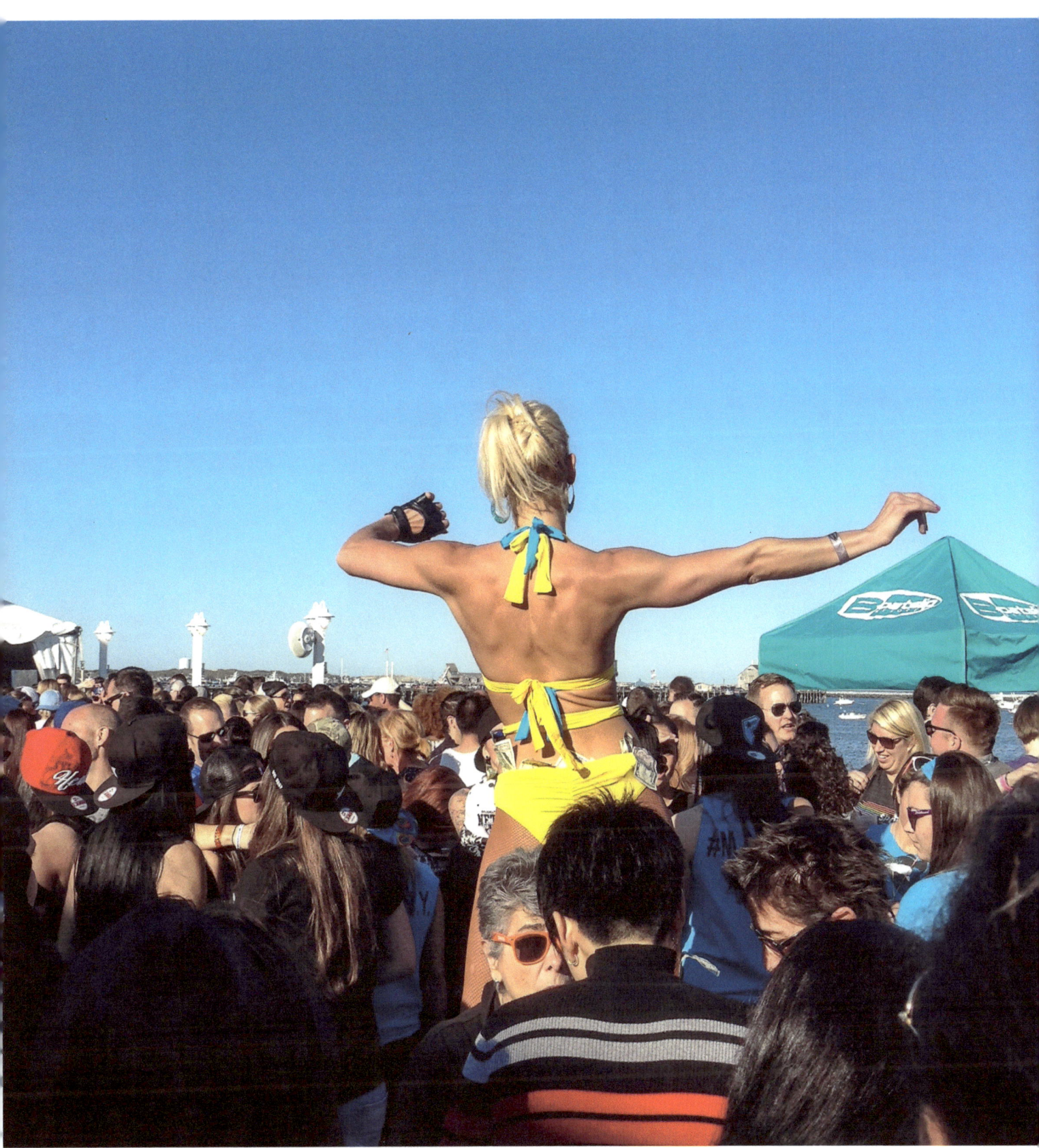

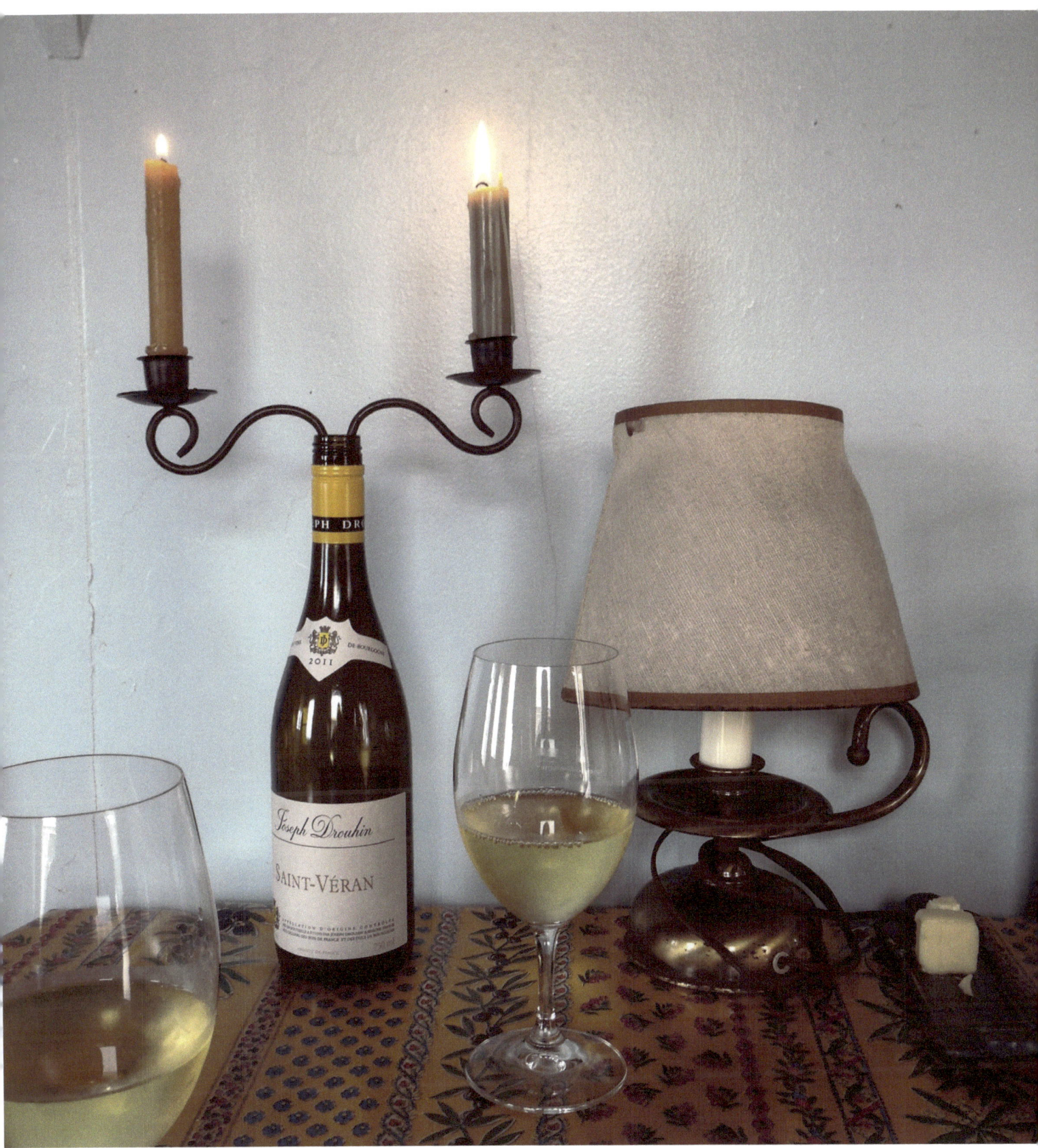

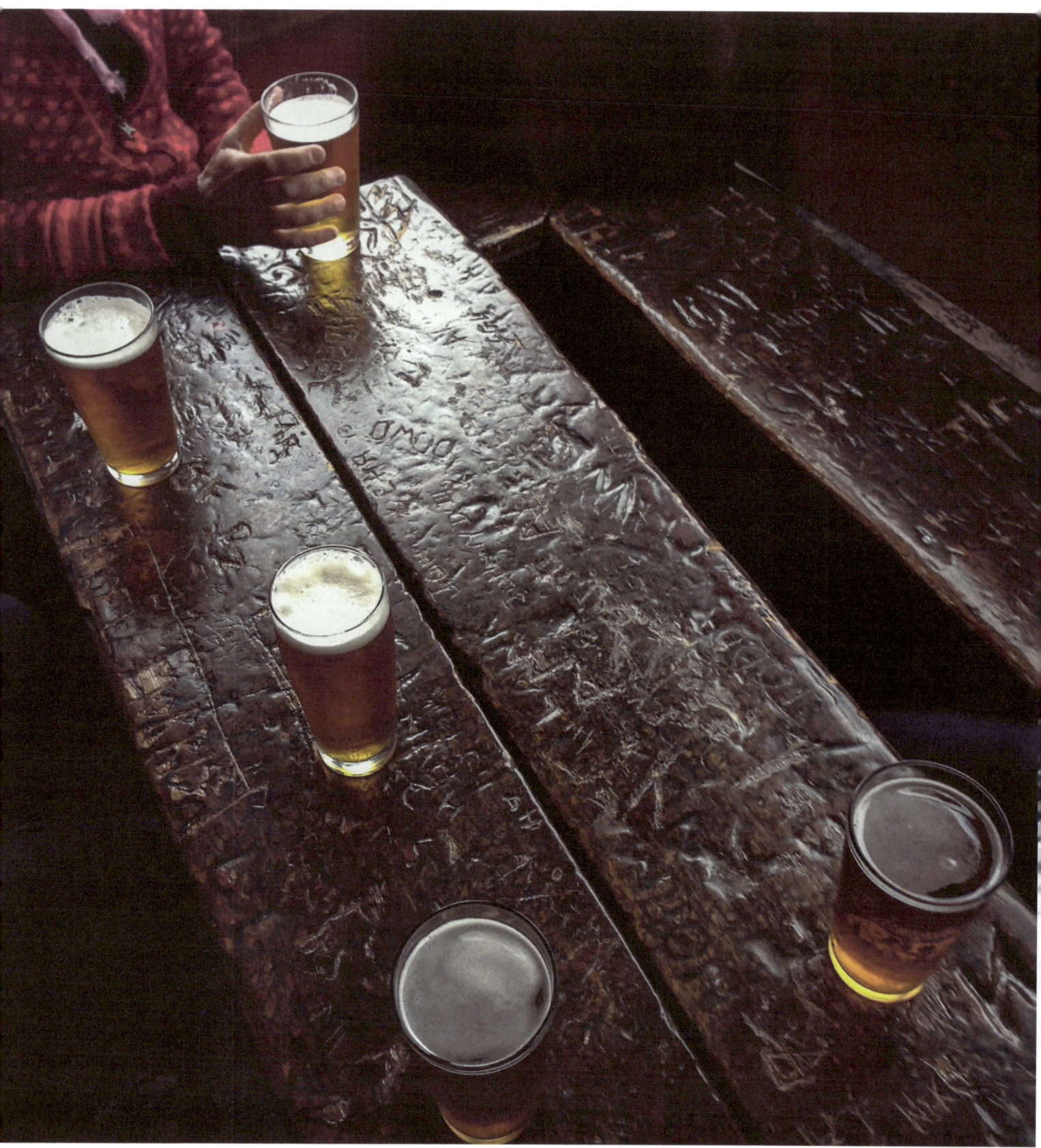

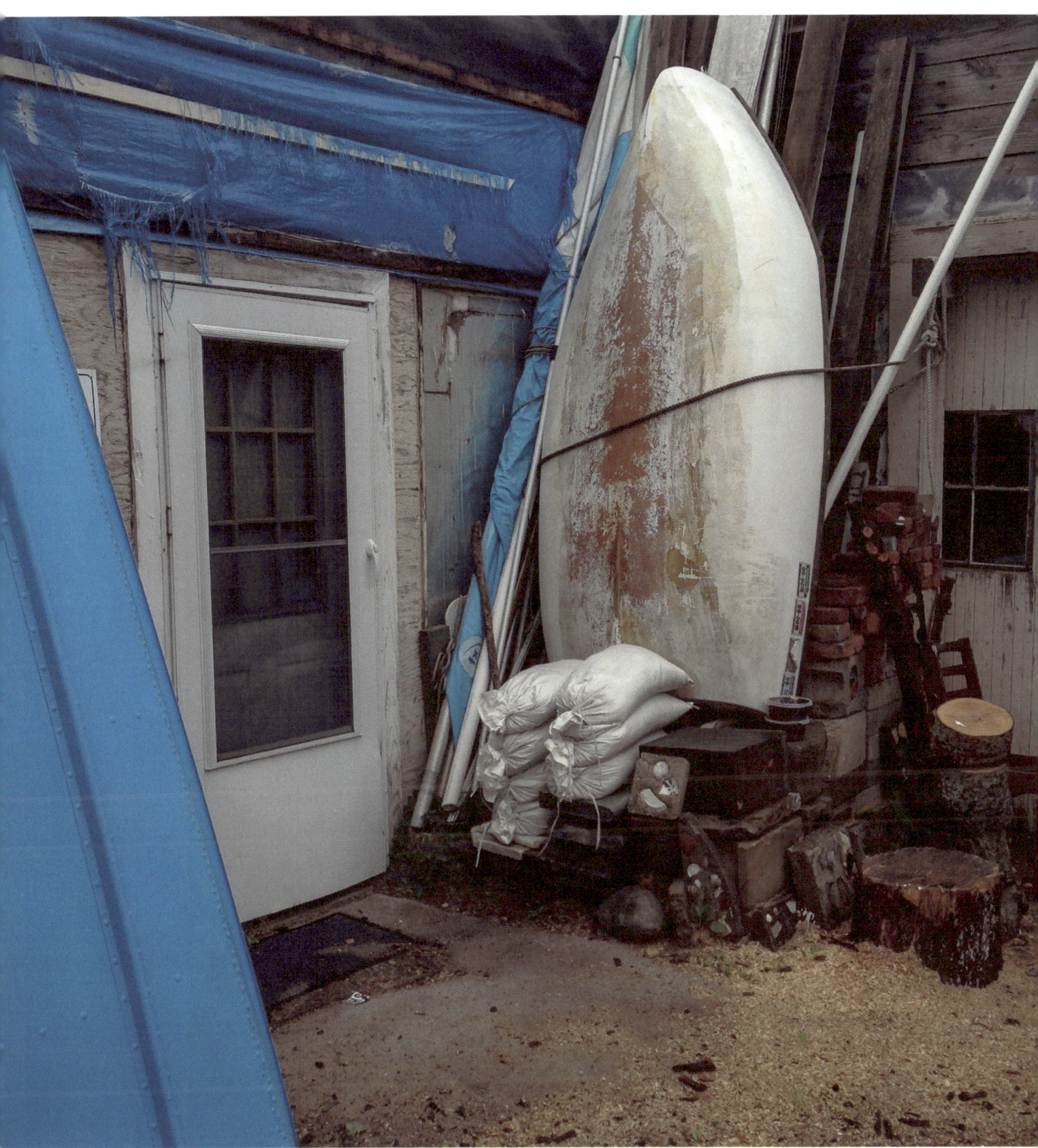

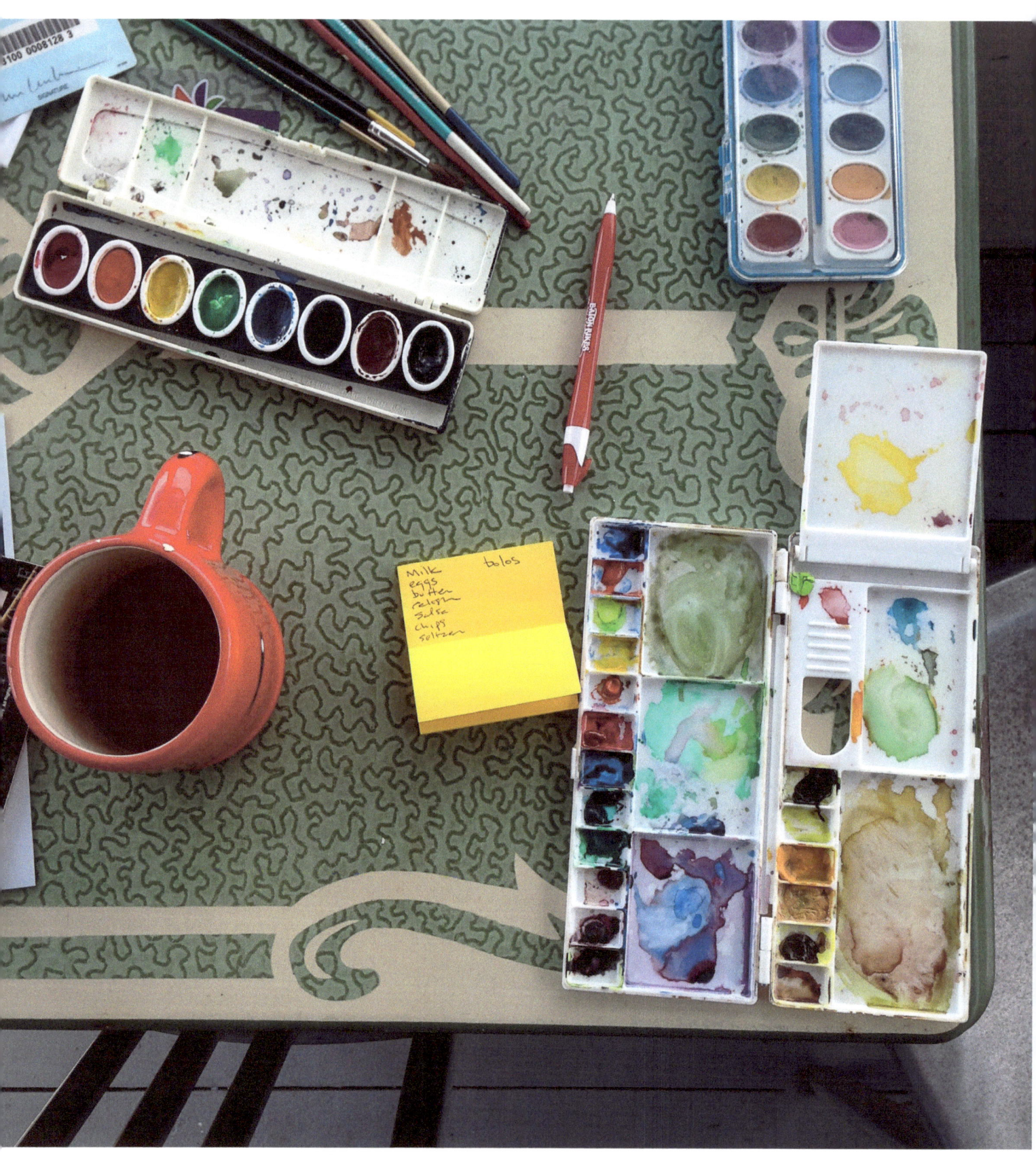

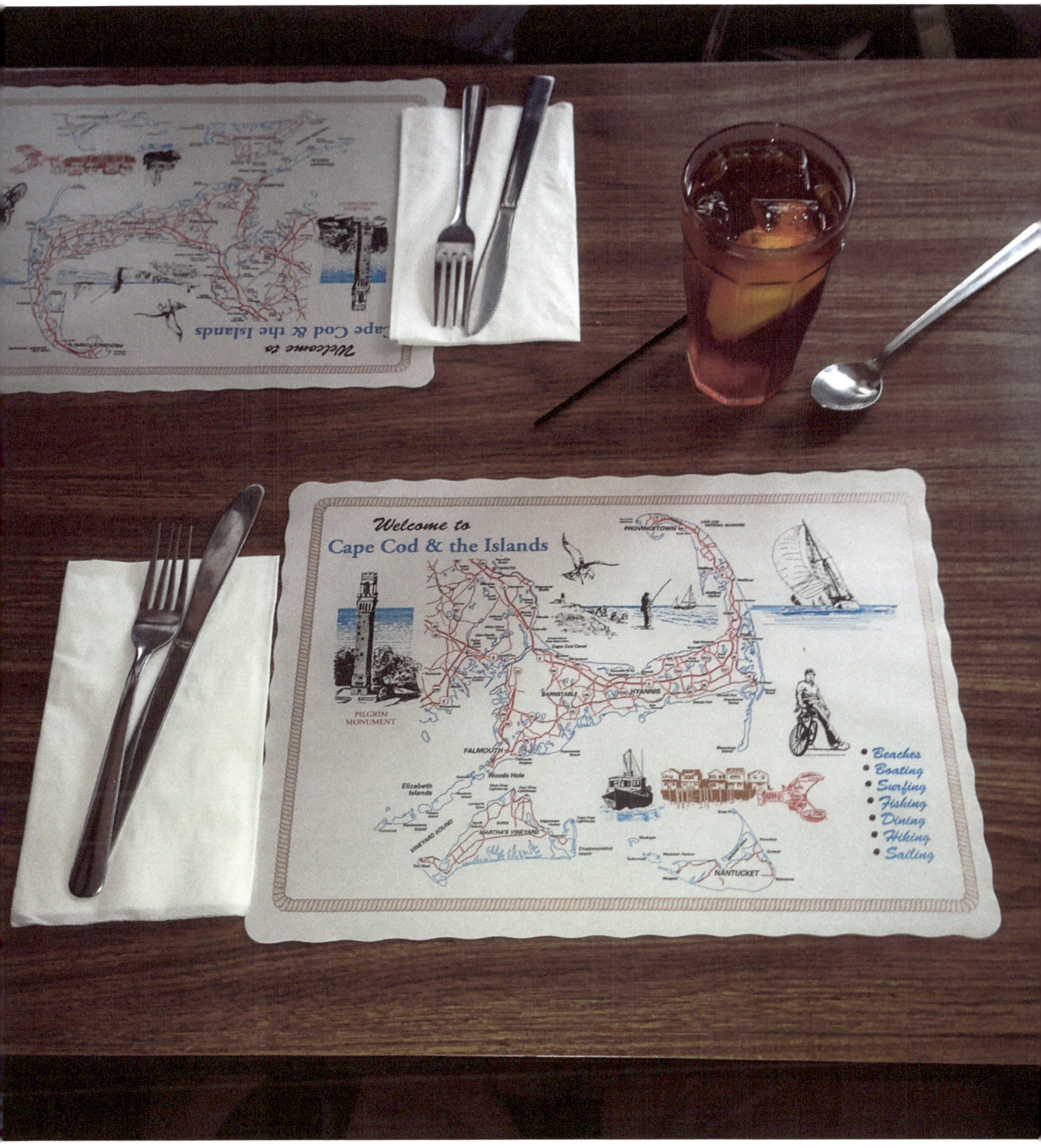

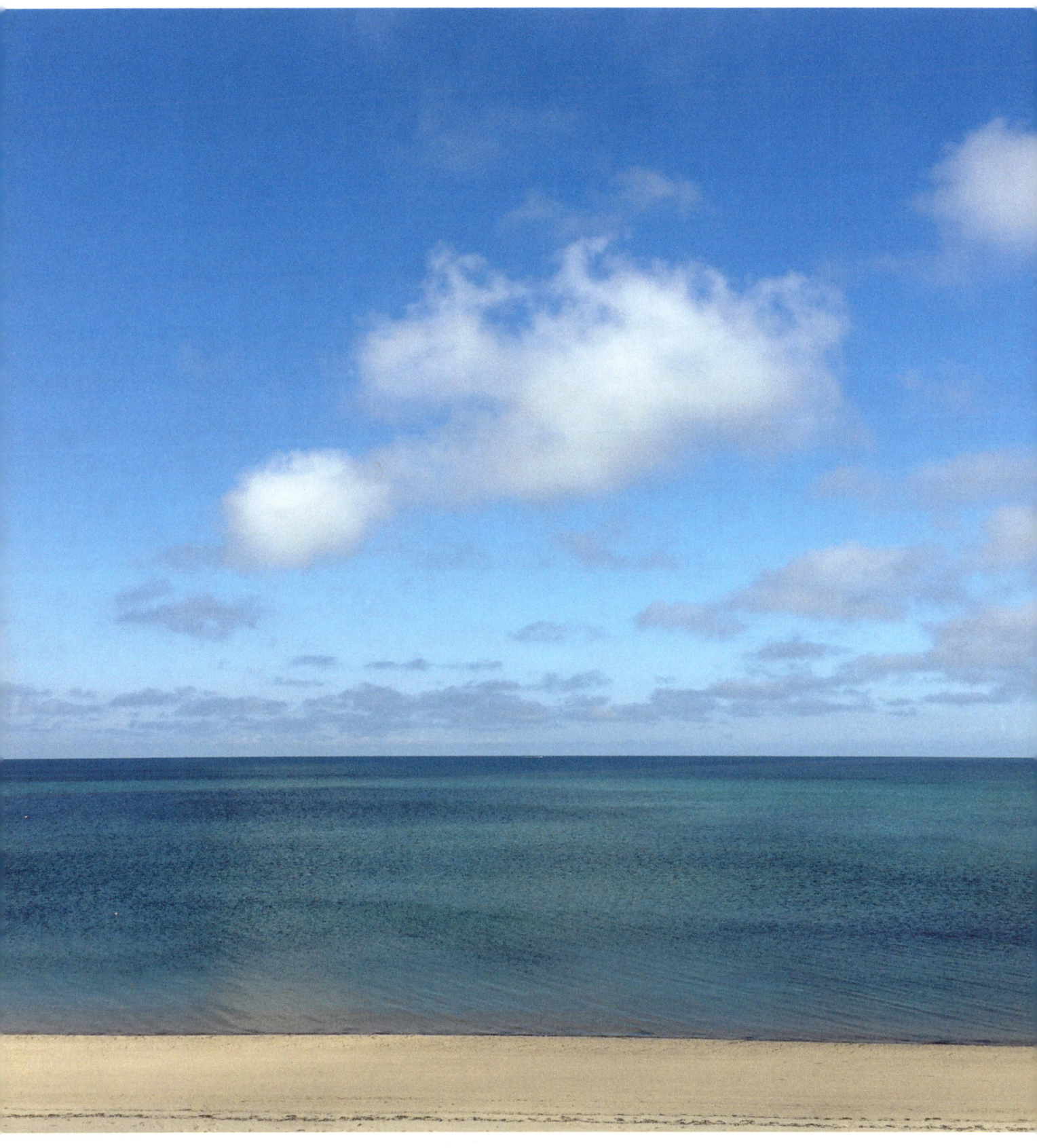

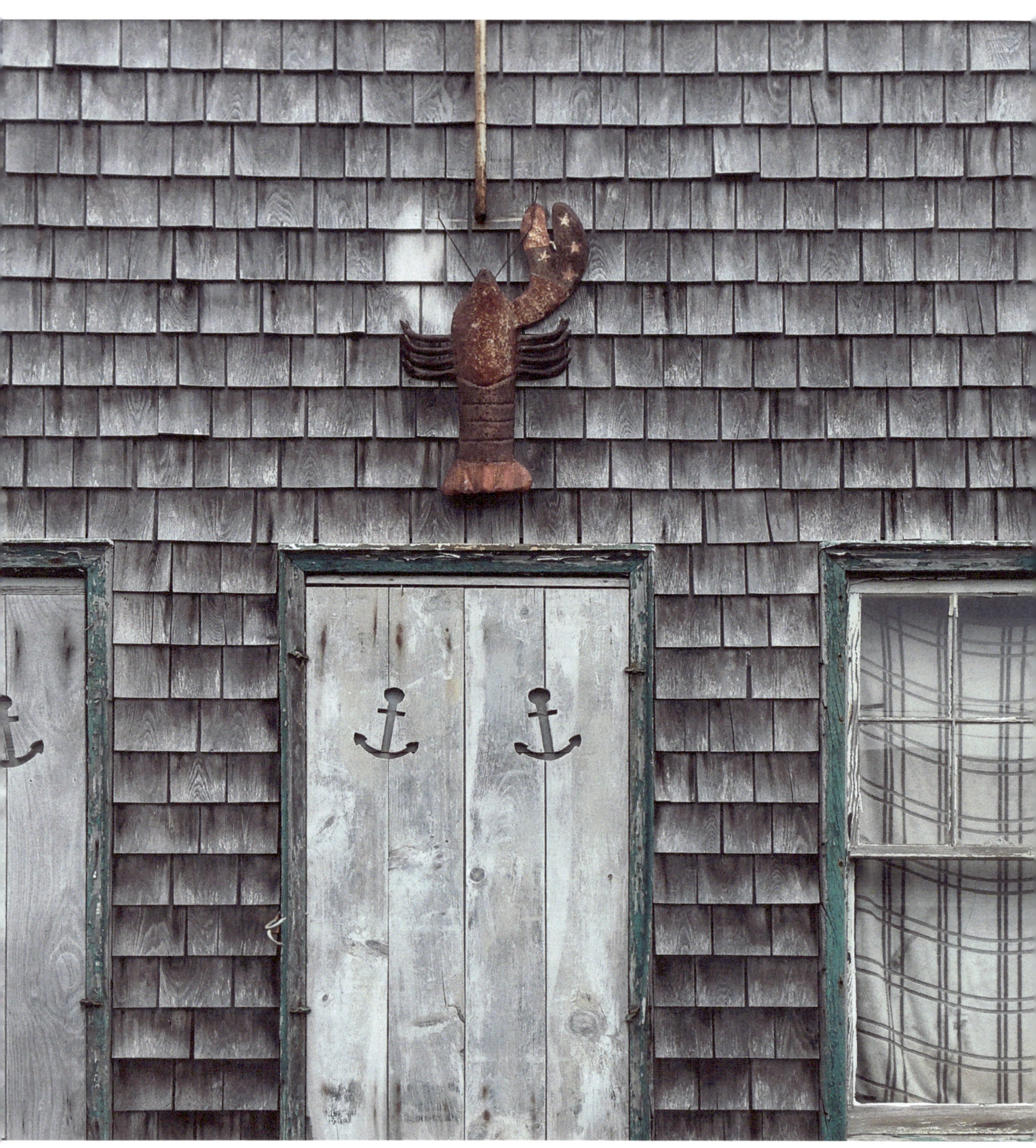

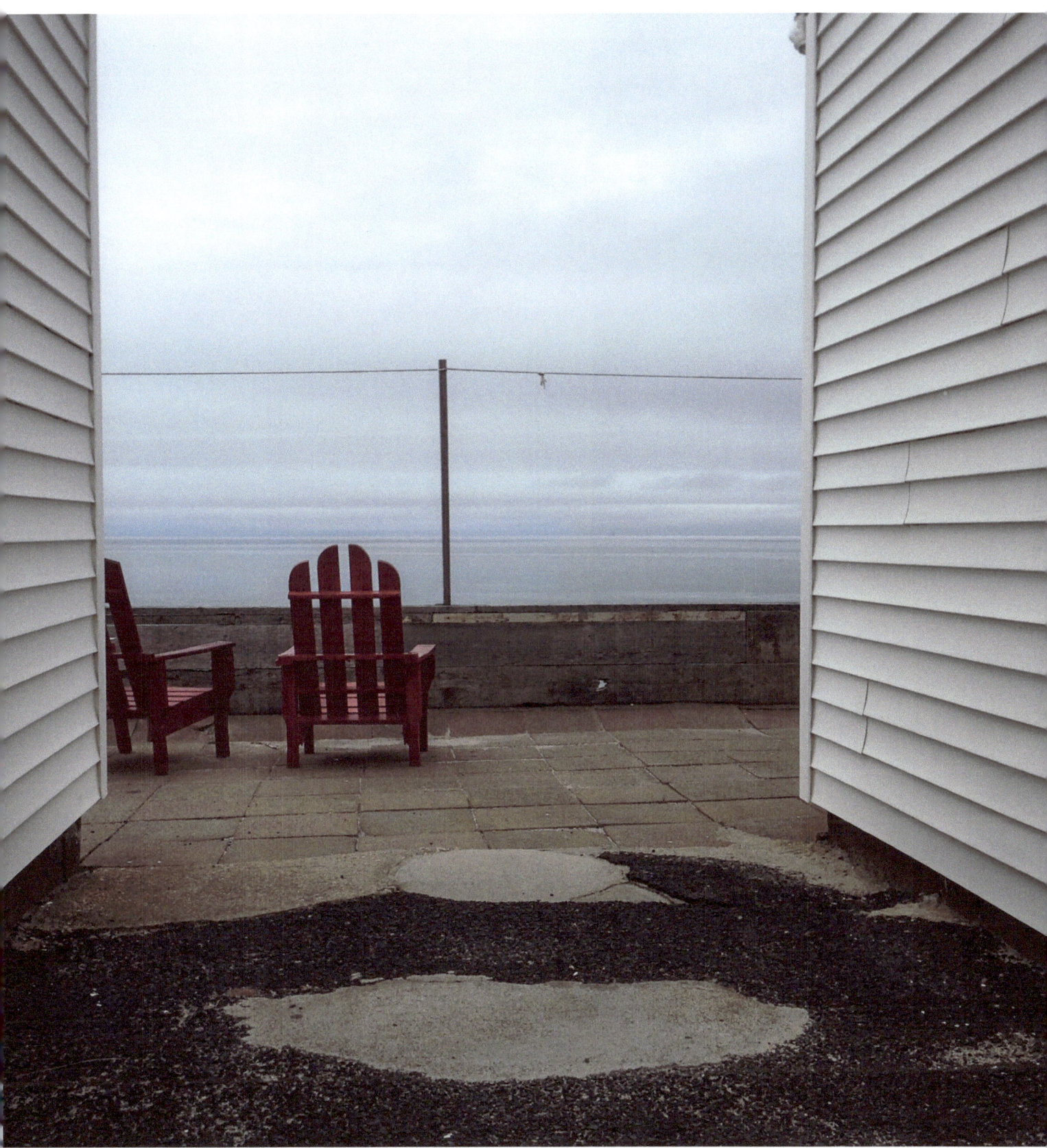

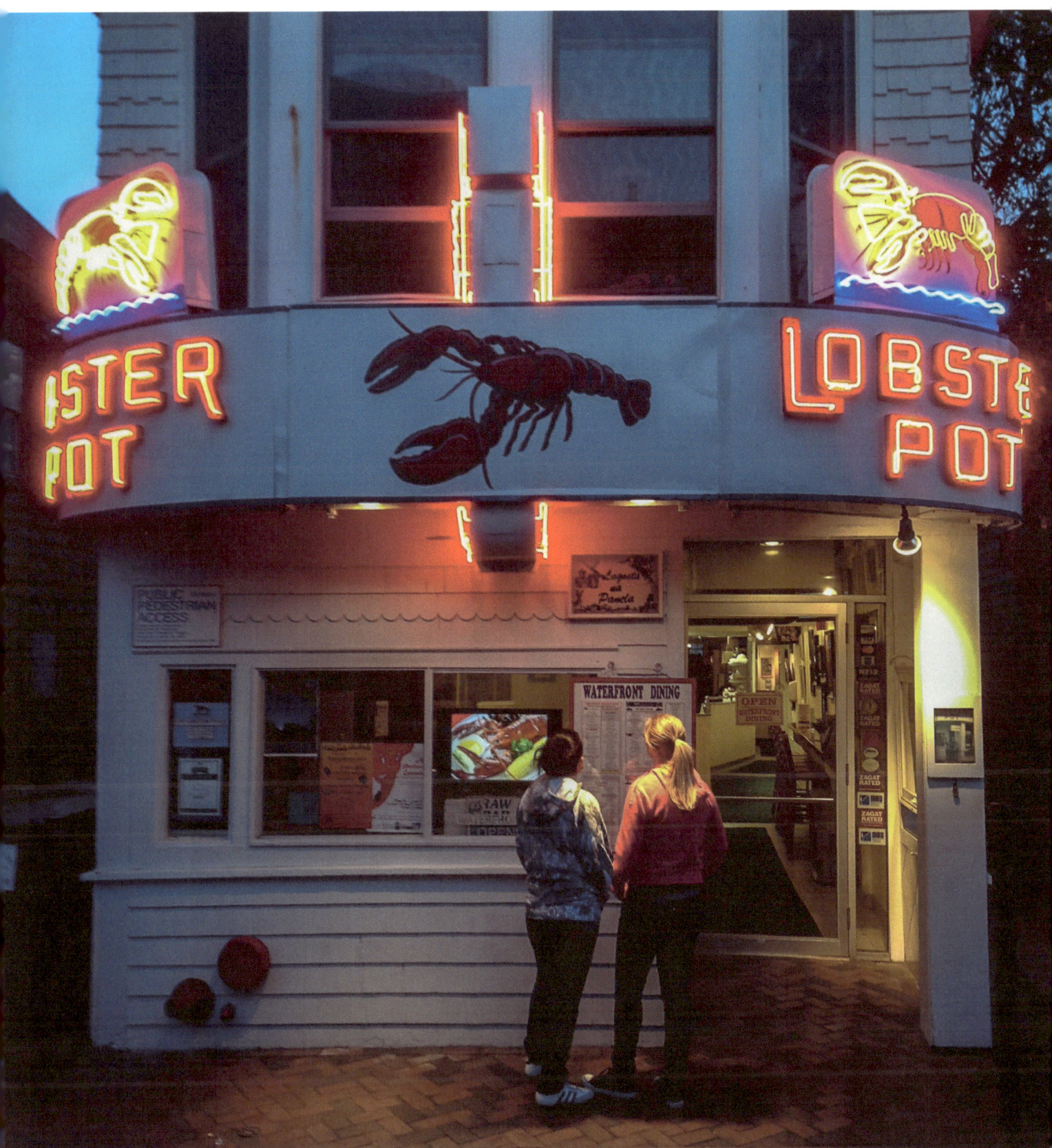

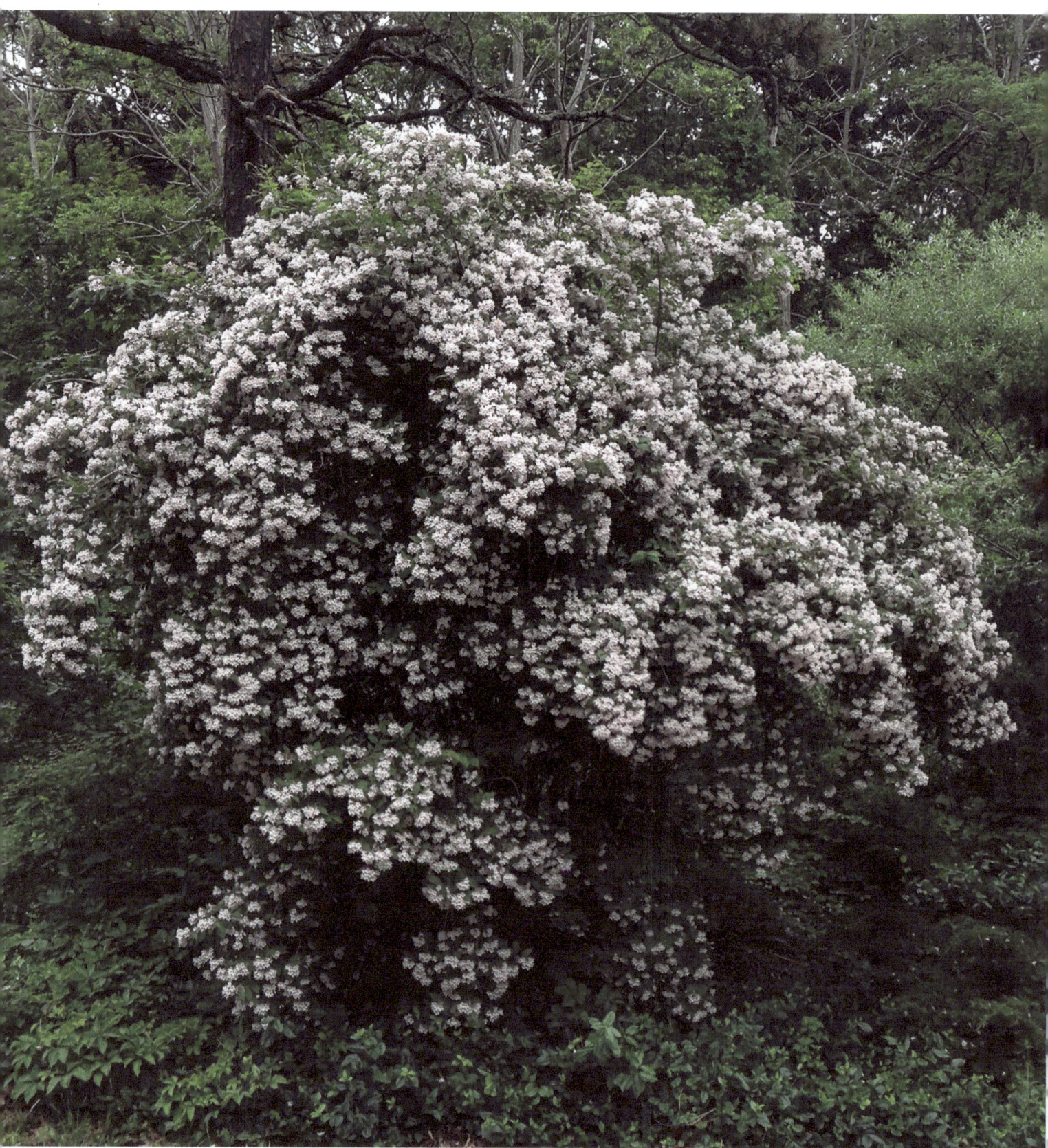

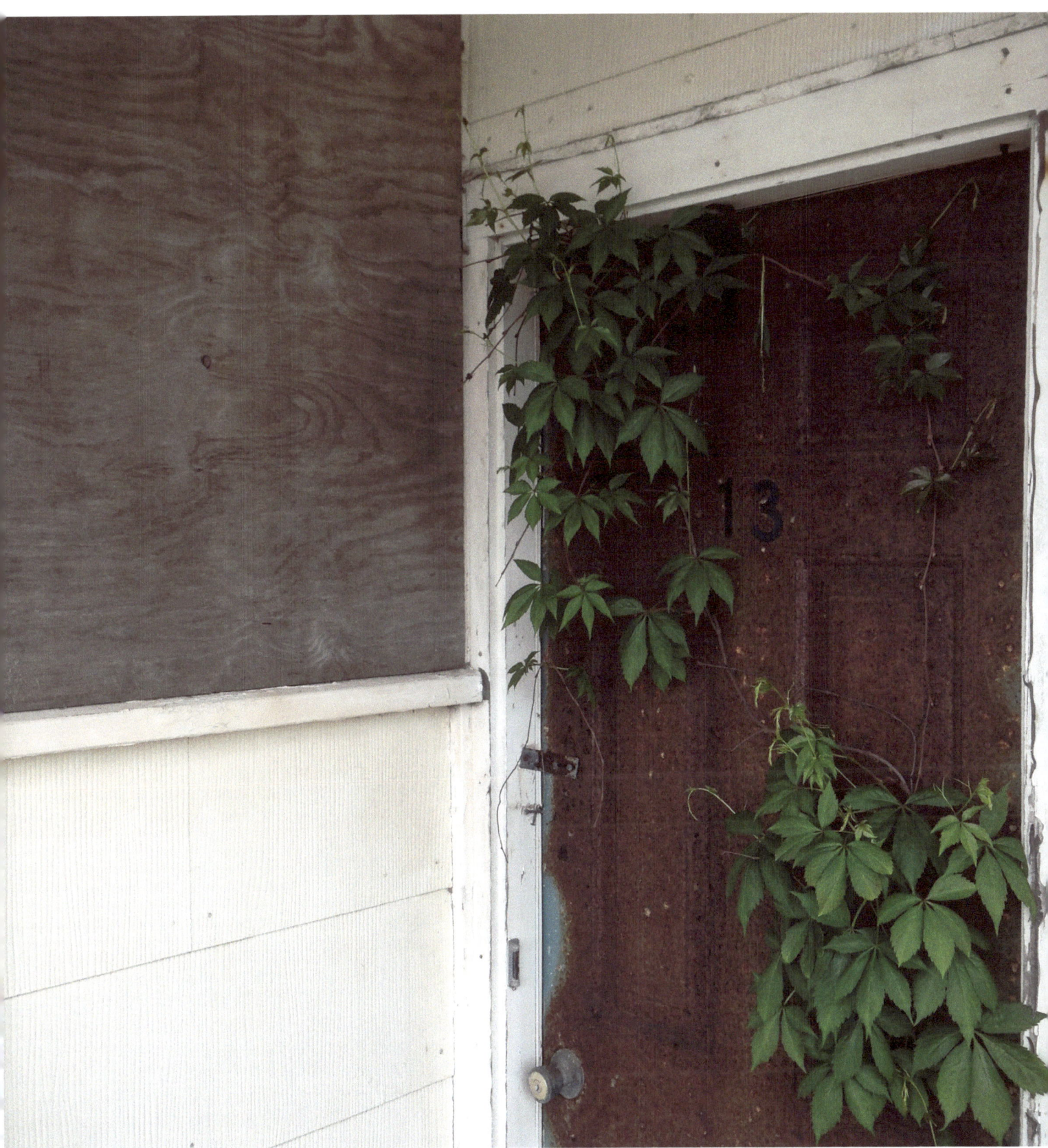

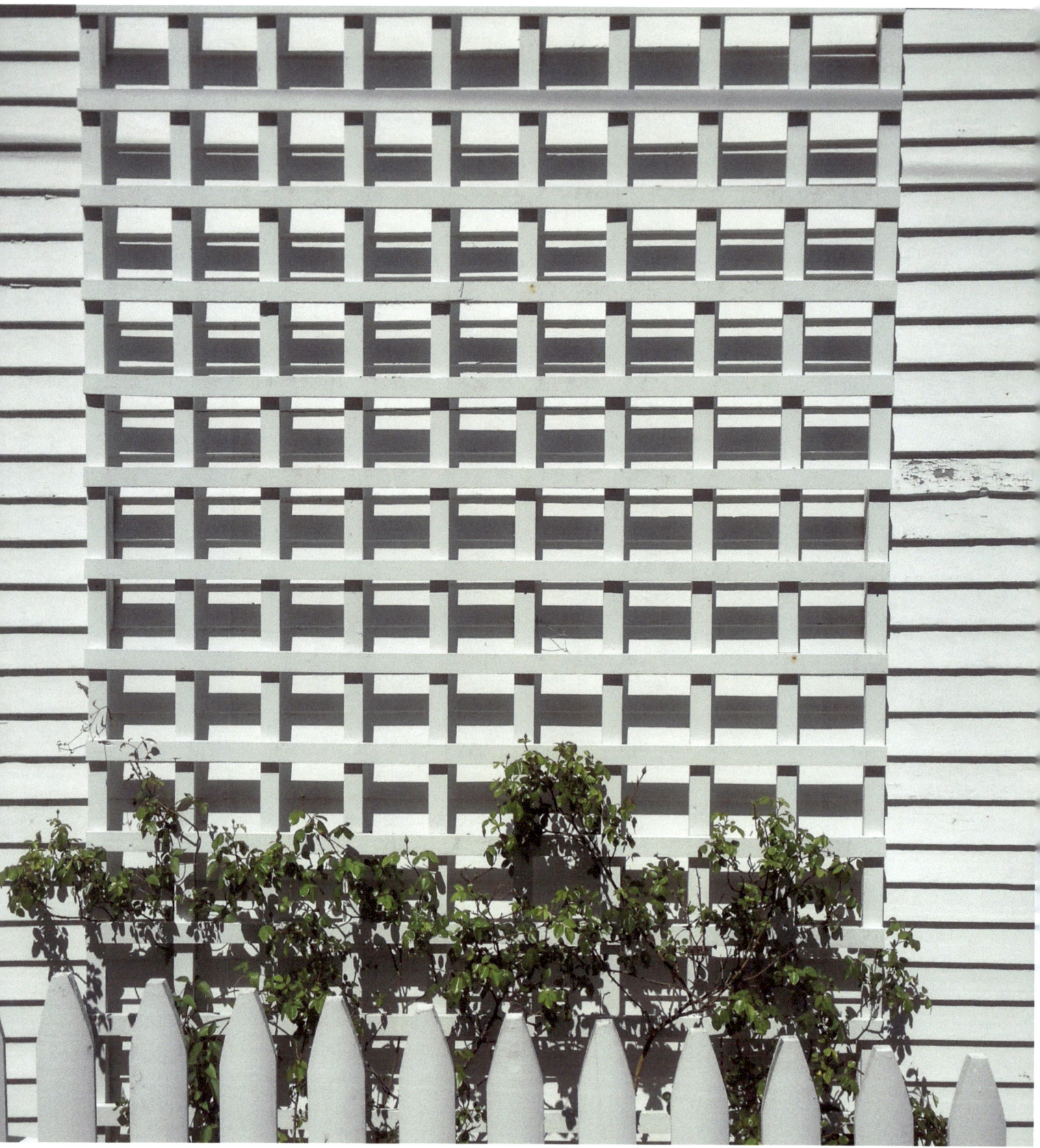

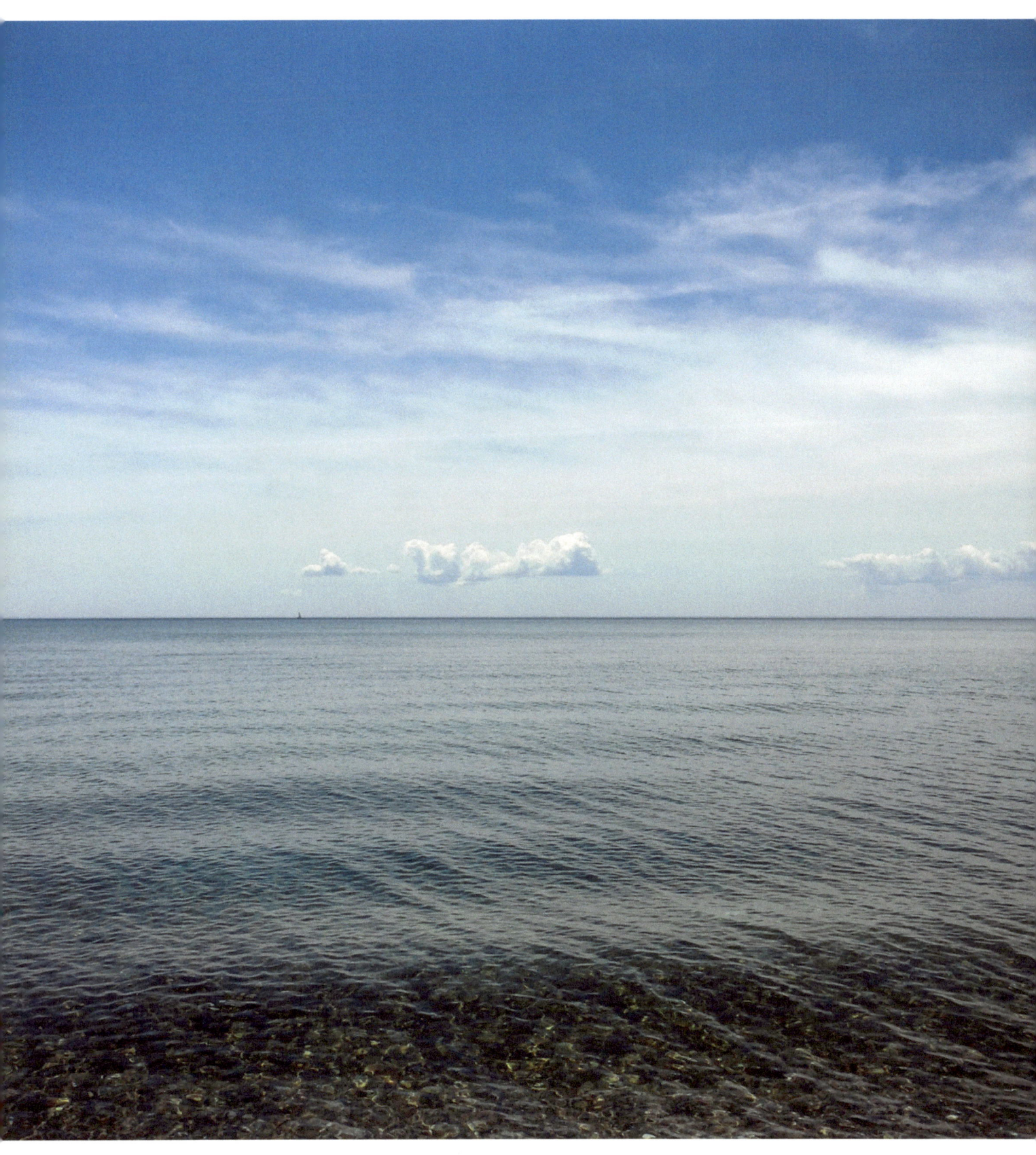

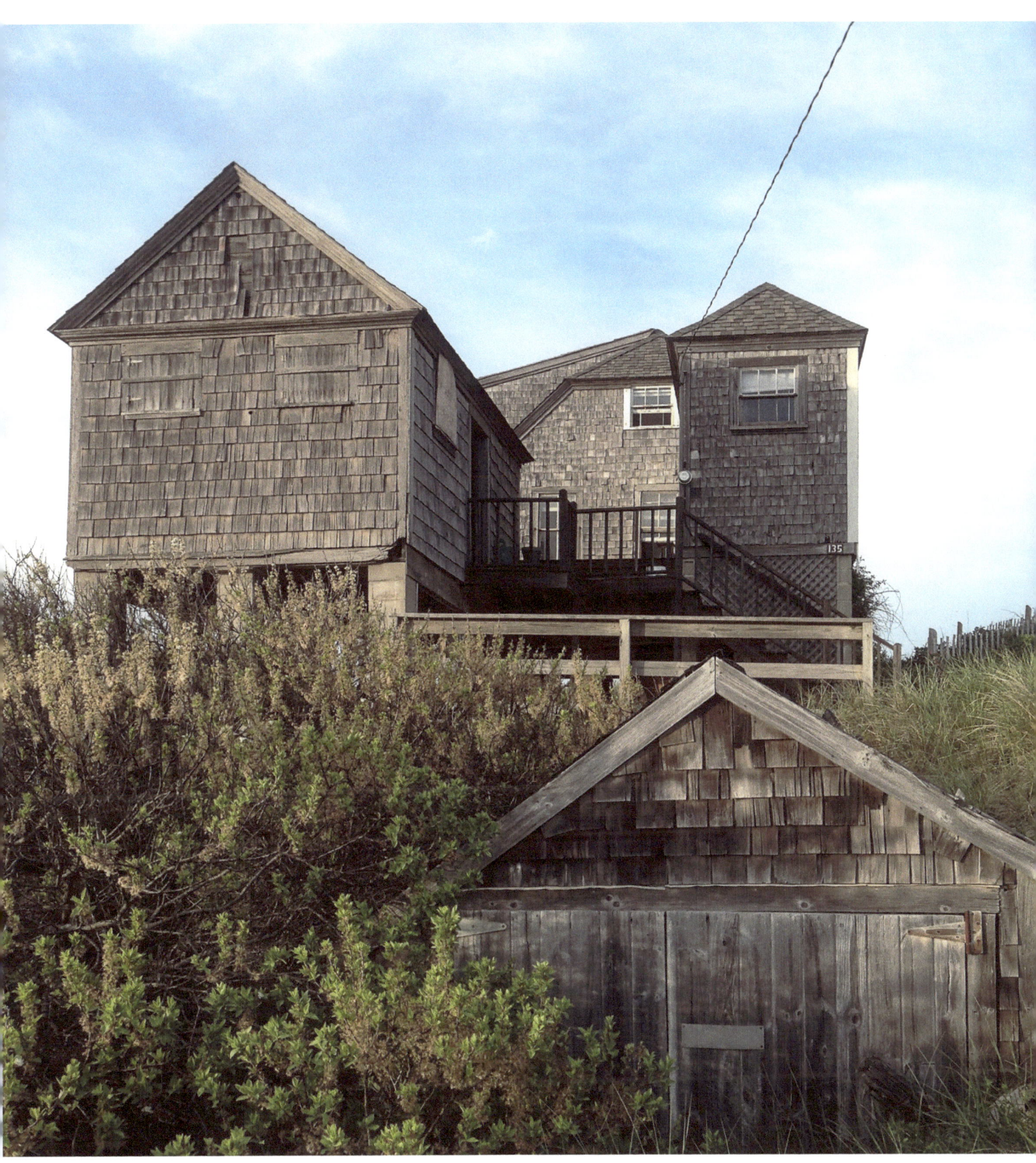

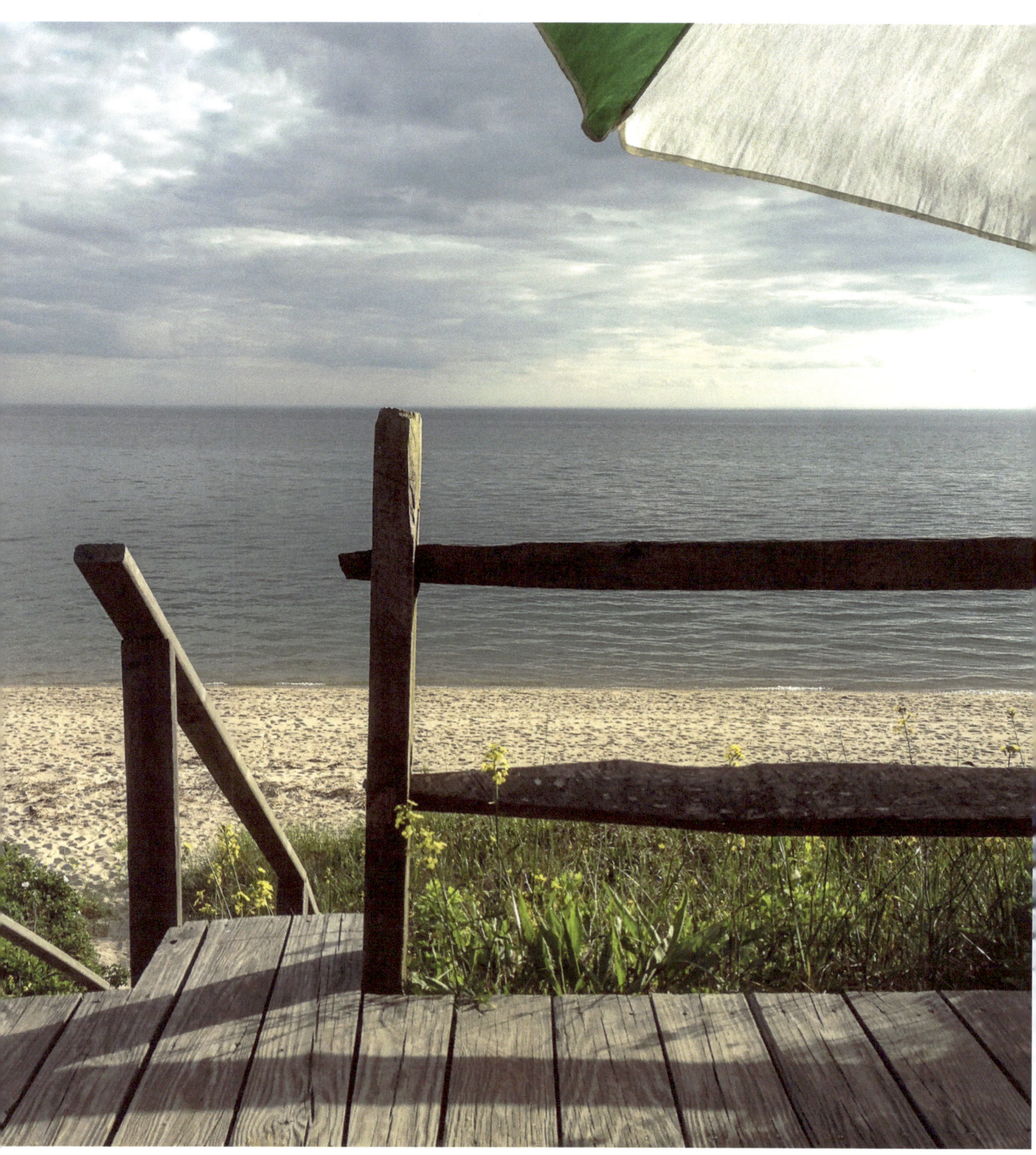

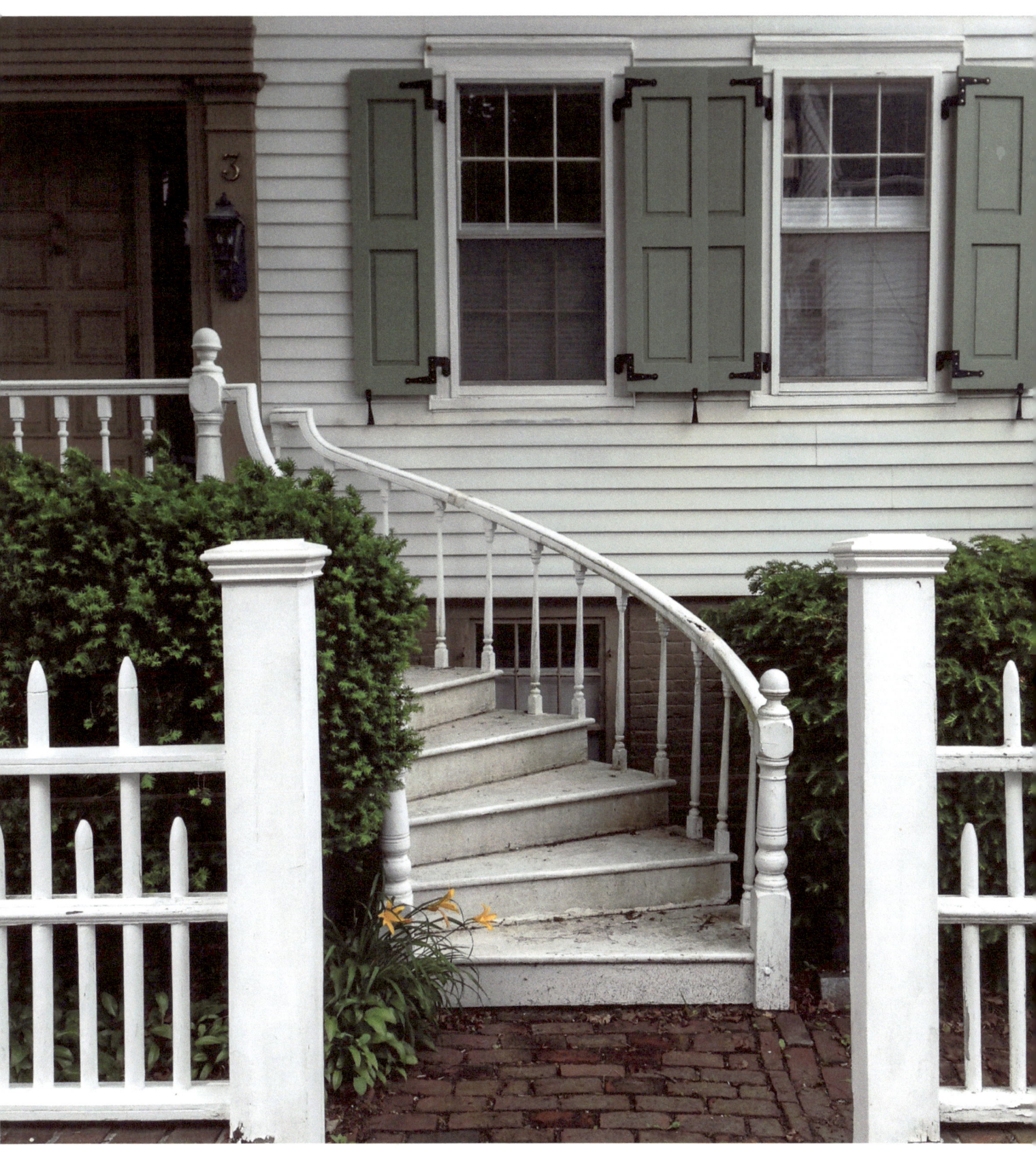

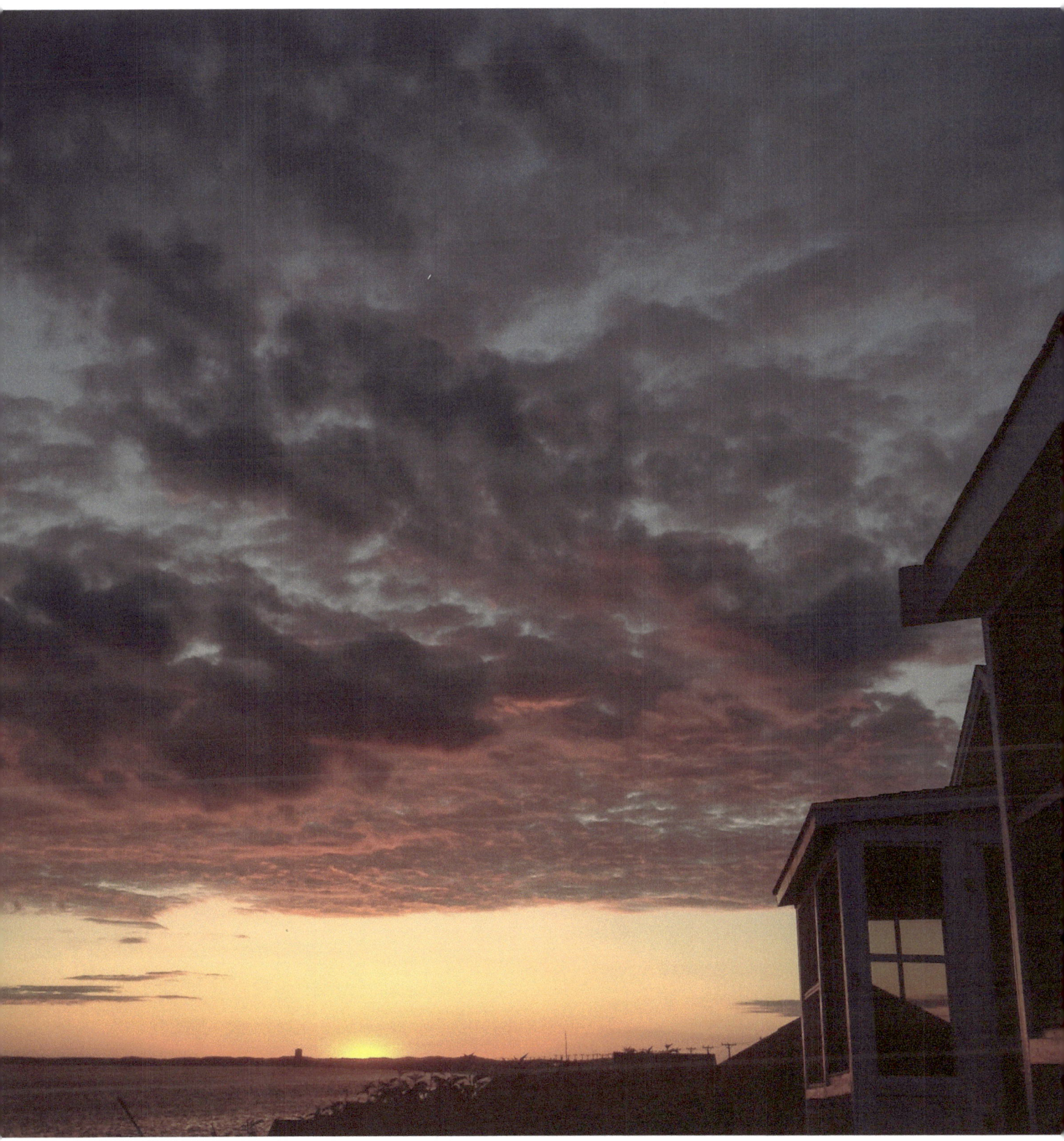

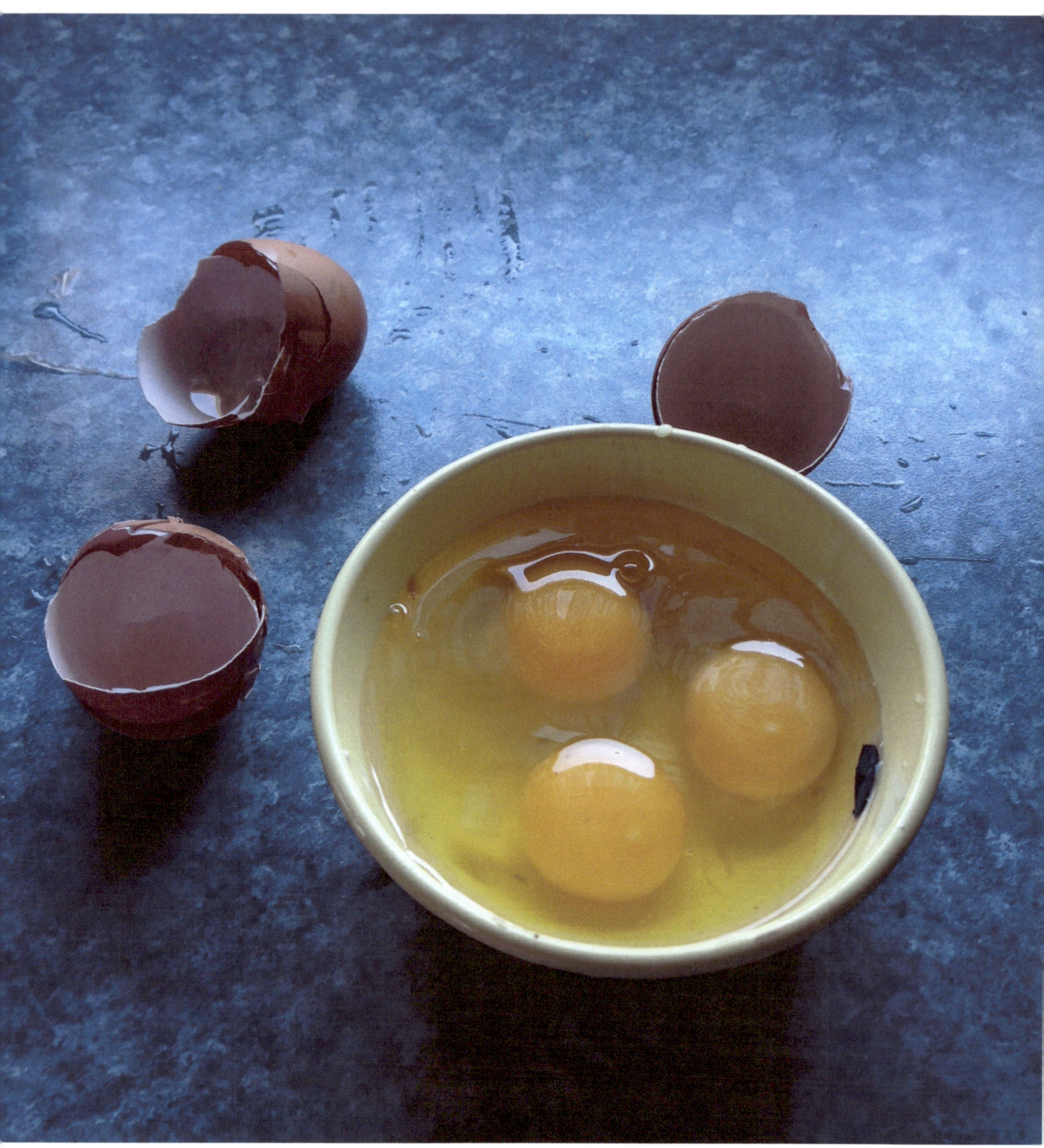

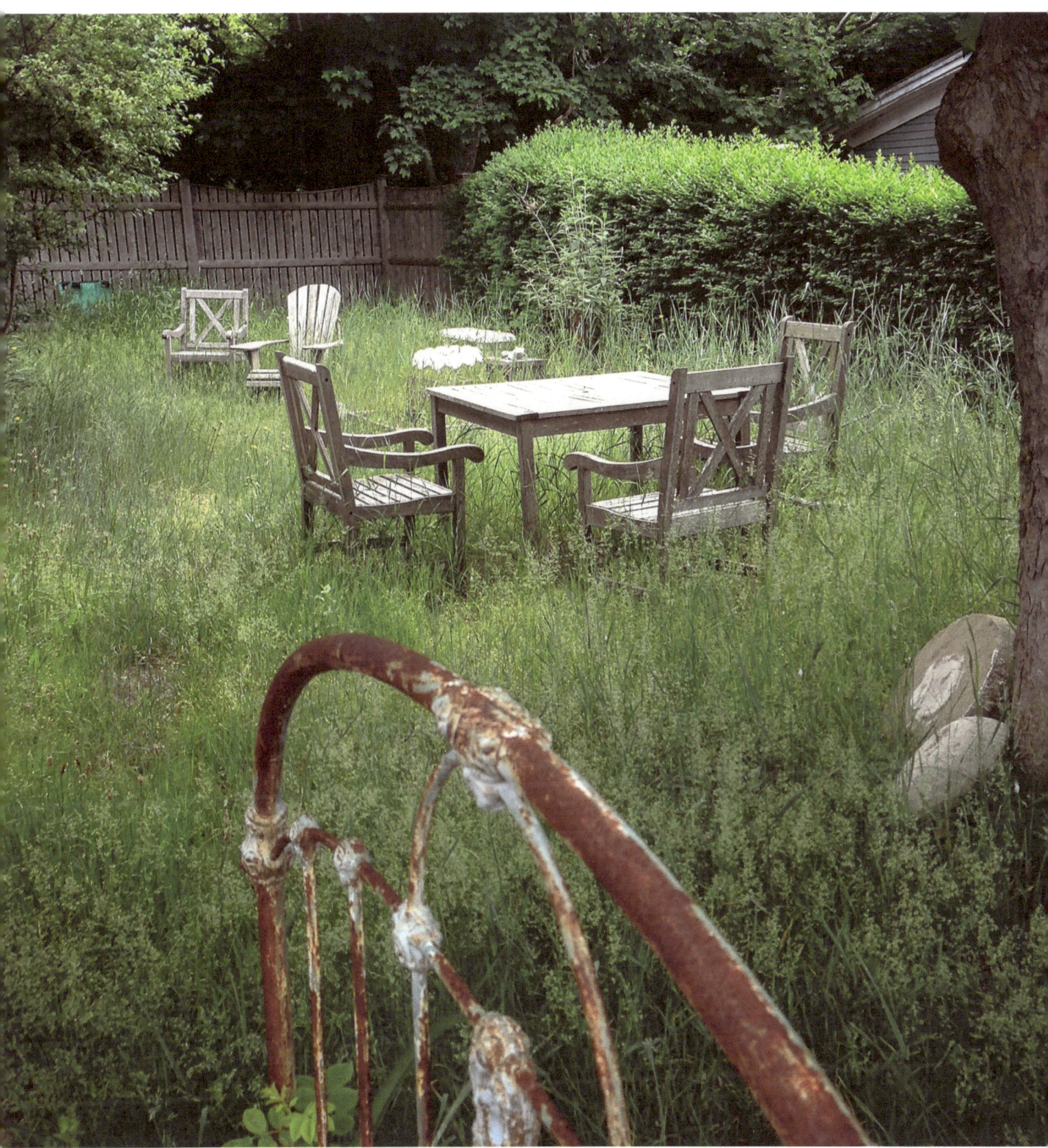

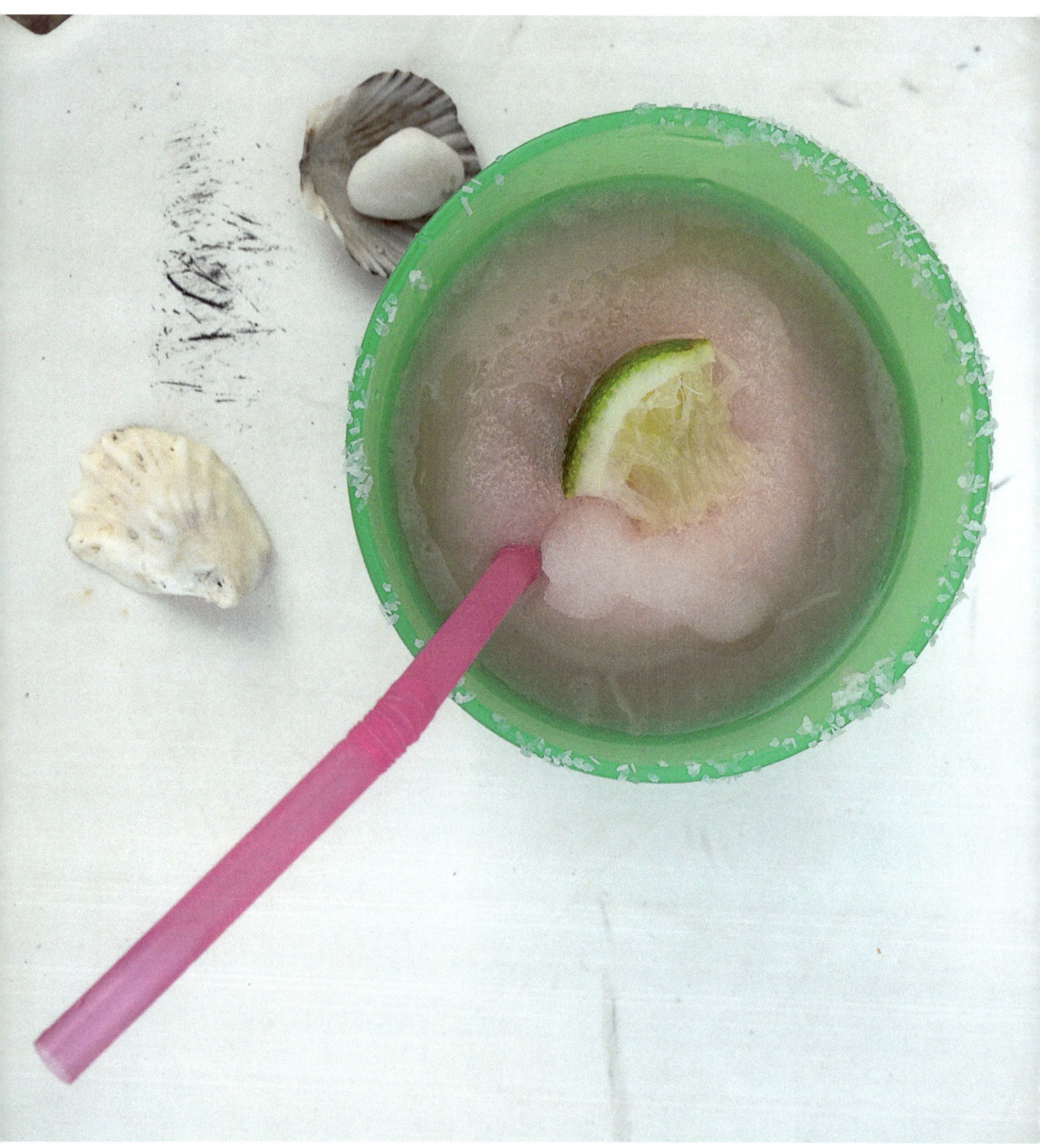

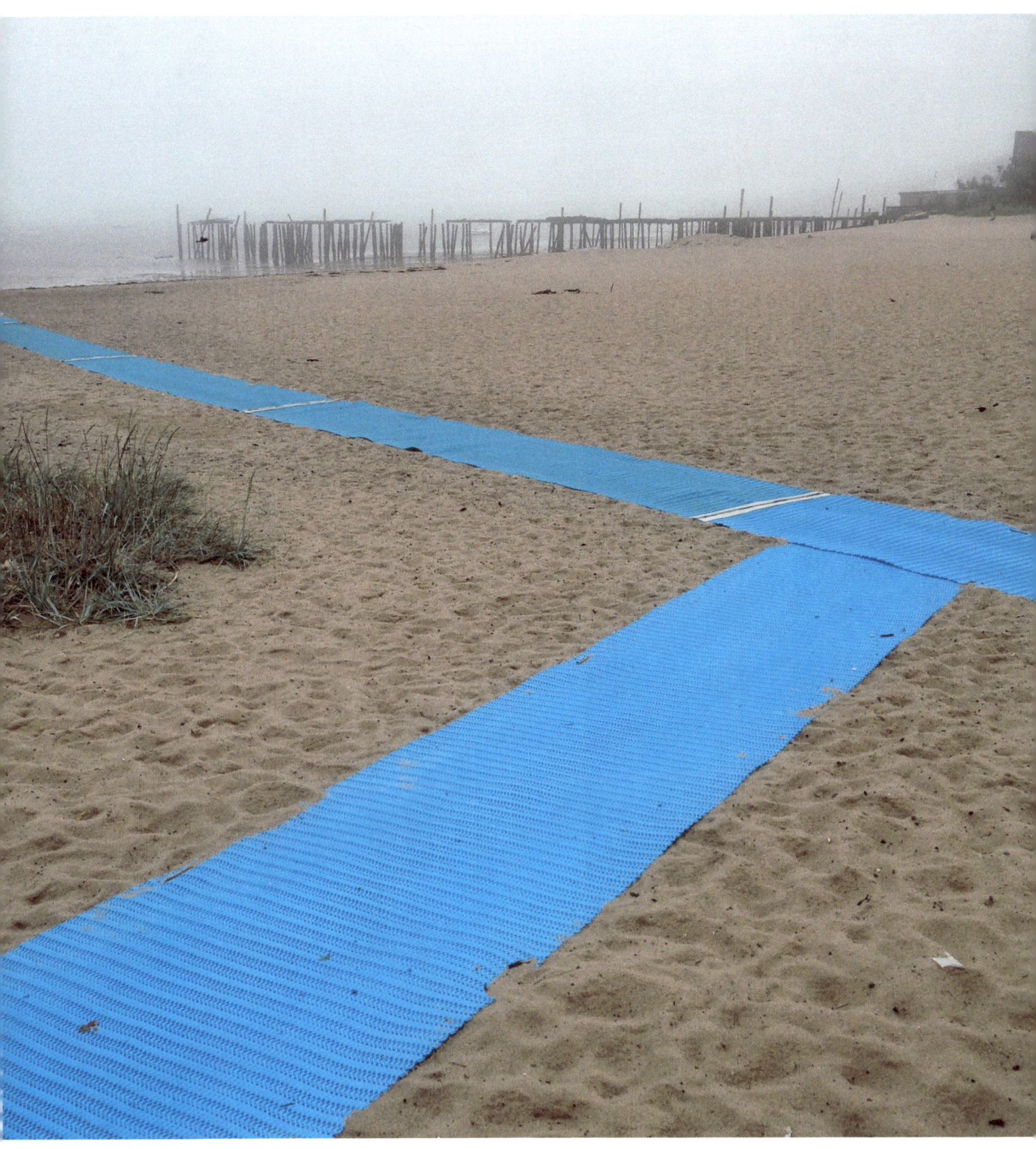

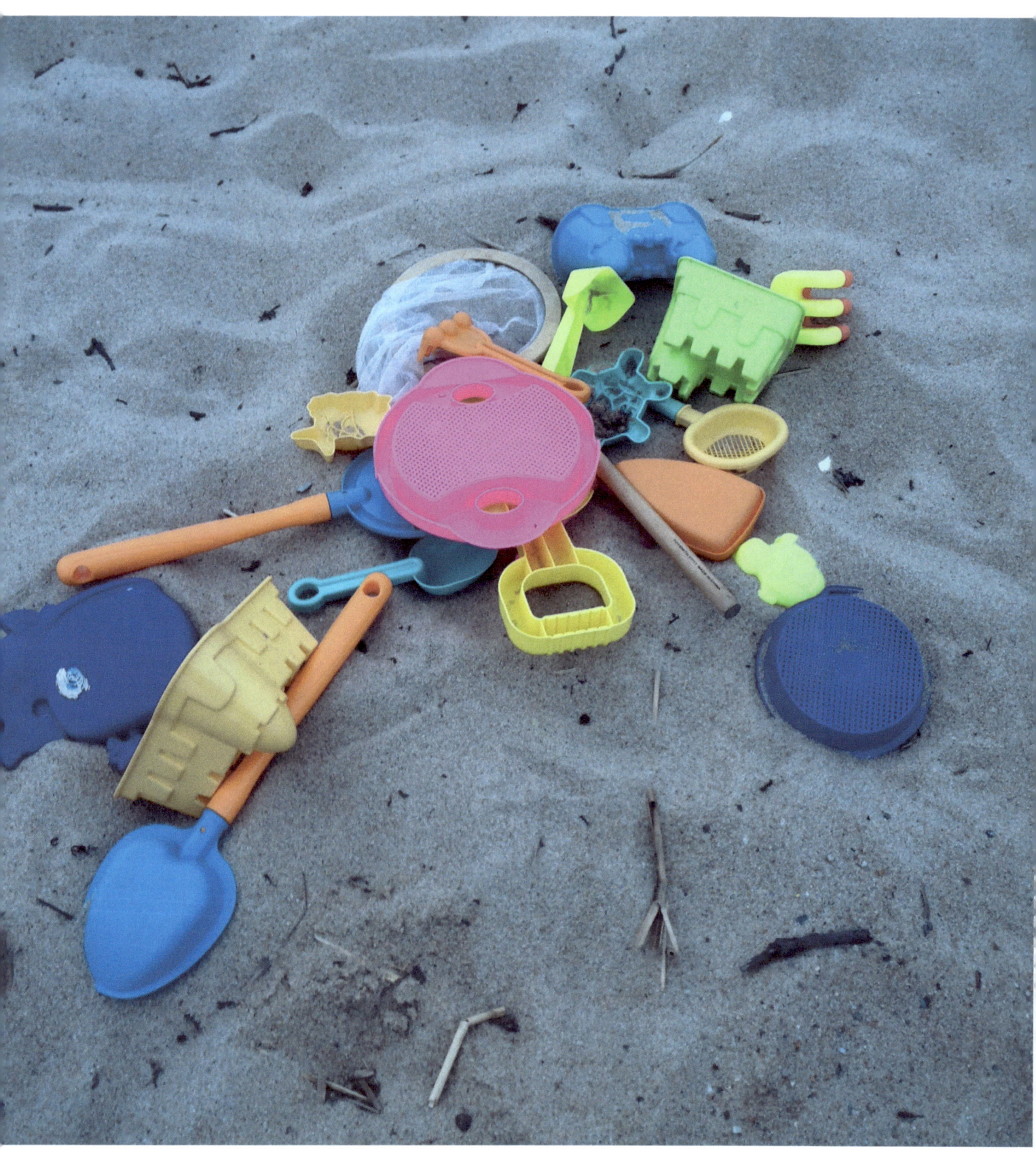

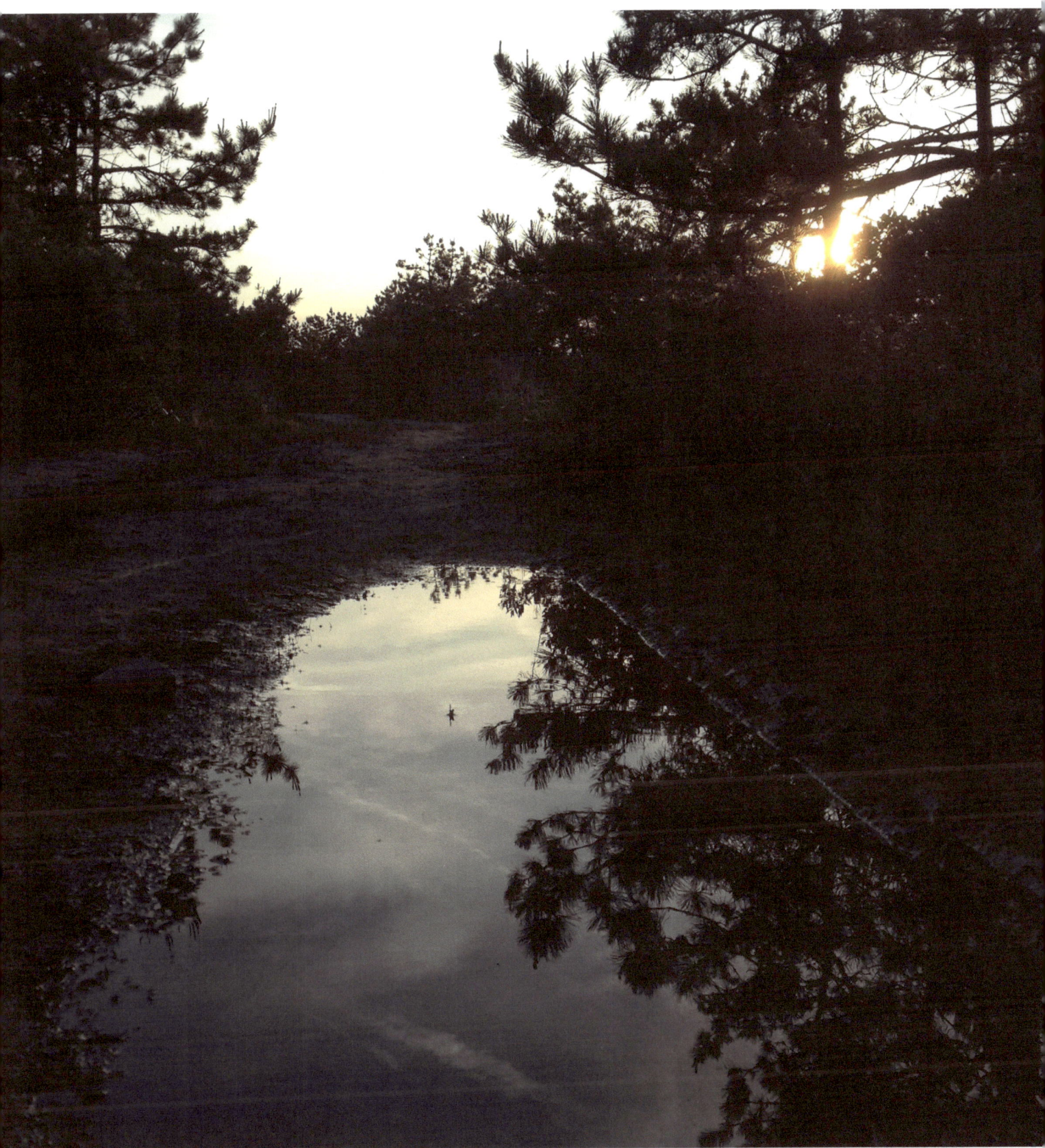

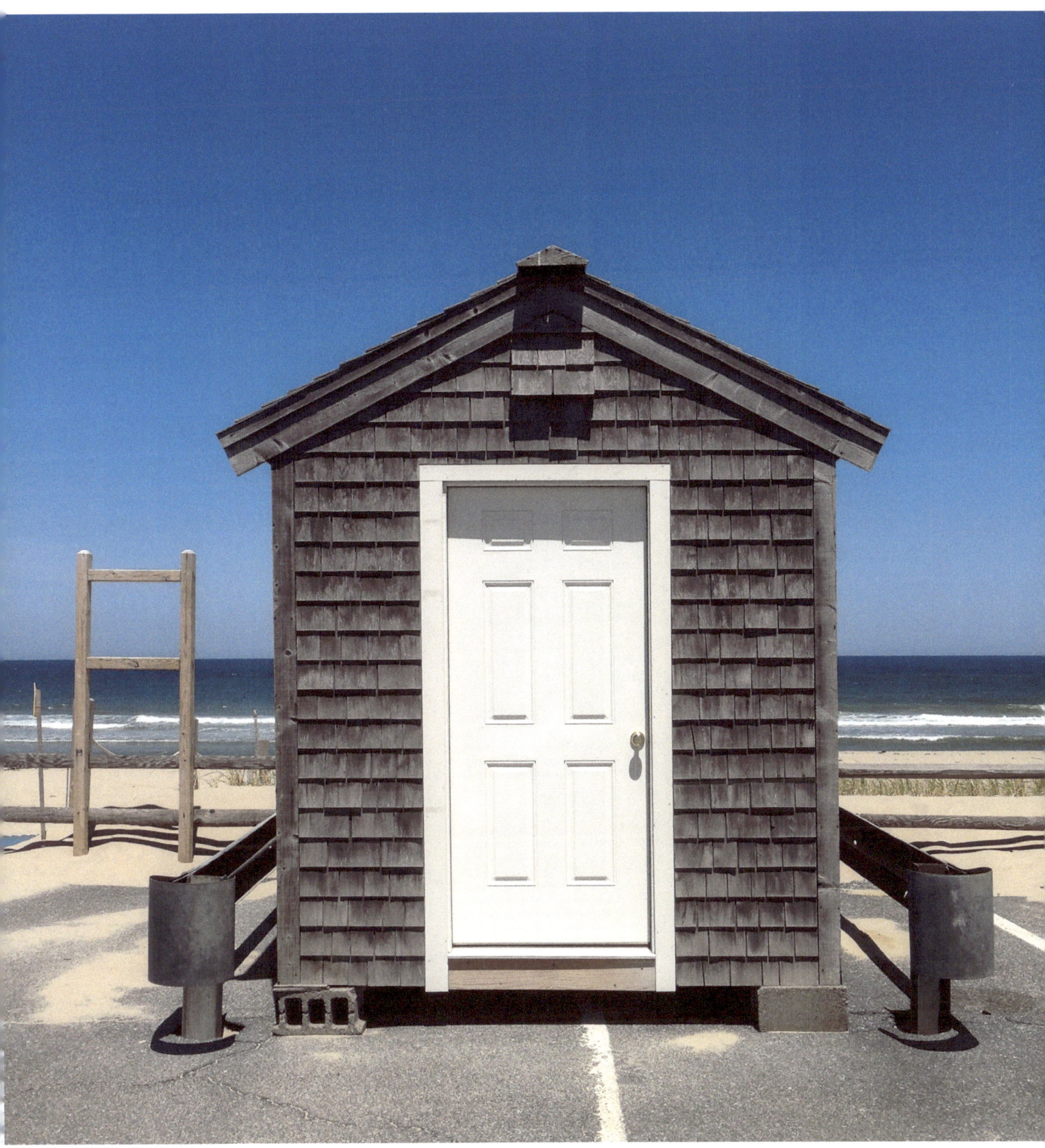

After many trips to Cape Cod, I finally discovered a place that had a sense of authenticity. It effectively fulfilled my romantic notion of what the Cape used to be like. Topside Cottages are situated on a bluff of sand and beach grass, overlooking Provincetown Harbor with Cape Cod Bay in the distance. One could simply refer to them as shacks on a hillside. As a matter of fact, a friend once said: cottage number 4 is pretty much a wooden tent but to me it's everything. These photographs were made with an iPhone 5 between May 22nd and June 13th, 2014 – my nineteenth year in the cottage.

Dan Larkin
dxlpph@rit.edu
instagram.com/the_larkman